OUTLOOK 2000

Copyright - Editions ENI - May 2001
ISBN: 2-7460-1226-X
Original edition: 2-7460-1169-7

ENI Publishing LTD

5 D Hillgate Place
18-20 Balham Hill
London SW12 9ER

Tel: 020 8673 3366
Fax: 020 8673 2277

e-mail: publishing@ediENI.com
http://www.eni-publishing.com

Collection directed by Corinne HERVO

MOUS
OUTLOOK 2000

OTHER FOLDERS

CONFIGURING OUTLOOK

SUMMARY EXERCISES

This book is the ideal tool for an effective preparation of the Outlook 2000 exam. The MOUS logo on the cover guarantees that this edition has been approved by Microsoft®. It contains the theoretical information corresponding to all the exam themes and you can test your knowledge by working through the practice exercises. If you succeed in completing these exercises without any difficulty, you are ready to take your exam. At the end of the book, you can see a list of the Outlook 2000 exam objectives, and the number of the lesson and exercise that refer to each of these objectives.

What is the Microsoft Office User Specialist certification?

The Microsoft Office User Specialist exam gives you the opportunity to obtain a meaningful certification, recognised by Microsoft®, for the Office applications: Word, Excel, Access, PowerPoint, and Outlook. This certification guarantees your level of skill in working with these applications. It can provide a boost to your career ambitions, as it proves that you can use effectively all the features of the Microsoft Office applications and thus offer a high productivity level to your employer. In addition, it would be a certain plus when job-seeking: more and more companies require employment candidates to be Microsoft Office User Specialist certificate holders.

What are the applications concerned?

You can gain Microsoft Office User Specialist certification in Office 97 applications (Word, Excel, PowerPoint and Access) and in Office 2000 applications (Word, Excel, PowerPoint, Access and Outlook). Microsoft Office User Specialist exams also exist for Word 7 and Excel 7. Two exam levels are offered for Word 97, Word 2000, Excel 97 and Excel 2000: a Core level (proficiency) and a second Expert level. For PowerPoint 97 and Access 97, only the Expert certification is available. For PowerPoint 2000, Access 2000 and Outlook 2000, only one level of certification is available.

INTRODUCTION
What is Microsoft Office User Specialist?

If you obtain the Expert level for Word 97, Excel 97, PowerPoint 97 and Access 97, you are certified as a Master in Office 97. If you obtain the Expert level for Word 2000 and Excel 2000 as well as Microsoft Office User Specialist certification in PowerPoint 2000, Access 2000 and Outlook 2000, you are certified as a Master in Office 2000.

How do you apply to sit the exams?

To enrol for the exams, you should contact one of the Microsoft Authorized Testing Centers (or ATC). A list of these centres is available online at this address: http://www.mous.net. Make sure you know for which version of the Office application you wish to obtain the certificate (is it the 97 or 2000 version?).

There is an enrolment fee for each exam.

On the day of the exam, you should carry some form of identification and, if you have already sat a Microsoft Office User Specialist exam, your ID number.

What happens during the MOUS exam?

During the exam, you will have a computer that you must use to perform a certain number of tasks on the software in question. Each action you perform to carry out these tasks will be tested in order to make sure that you have done correctly what was asked of you.

You are allowed no notes, books, pencils or calculators during the exam. You can consult the application help, but you should be careful not to exceed the exam's time limit.

Each exam is timed; it lasts in general between 45 minutes and one hour.

How do you pass the exam?

You must carry out a certain percentage of the required tasks correctly, within the allocated time. This percentage varies depending on the exam.

You will be told your result as soon as you have finished your exam. These results are confidential (the data are coded) and are only made known to the candidate and to Microsoft.

What happens then?

You will receive a Microsoft-approved exam certificate, proving that you hold the specified Microsoft Office User Specialist level.

How this book works

This book is the ideal companion to an effective preparation of the **MOUS Outlook 2000** exam. It is divided into several sections, each containing one or more **chapters**. Each section deals with a specific topic: the Outlook working environment, email (sending, receiving and managing messages) the Calendar, the Contacts, Tasks and Notes folder and Outlook configuration. Each chapter is independent from the others. You can work according to your needs: if you already know the techniques for working with records, for example, you can skip this lesson and go straight to the practice exercise for that chapter, then if you feel you need some extra theory, you can look back at the relevant points in the lesson. You can also study the lesson and/or work through the exercises in any order you wish.

At the end of the book, there is an **index** to help you find the explanations for any action, whenever you need them.

From theory...

Each chapter starts with a **lesson** on the theme in question and the lesson is made up of a variable amount of numbered topics. The lesson should supply you with all the theoretical information necessary to acquire that particular skill. Example screens to illustrate the point discussed enhance the lesson and you will also find tips, tricks and remarks to complement the explanations provided.

...To practice

Test your knowledge by working through the **practice exercise** at the end of each chapter: each numbered heading corresponds to an exercise question. A solution to the exercise follows. Some of these exercises are done using documents on the CD-ROM accompanying the book, that you install on your own computer (to see how, refer to the INSTALLING THE CD-ROM instructions). In addition to the chapter exercises, five **summary exercises** dealing with each of the section themes are included at the end of the book.

All you need to succeed!

When you can complete all the practice exercises without any hesitation or problems, you are ready to sit the Microsoft Office User Specialist exam. In the table of contents for each chapter, the topics corresponding to a specific exam objective are marked with this symbol: ▦. At the back of the book, you can also see **the official list of the Outlook 2000 exam objectives** and for each of these objectives the corresponding lesson and exercise number.

The layout of this book

This book is laid out in a specific way with special typefaces and symbols so you can find all the information you need quickly and easily:

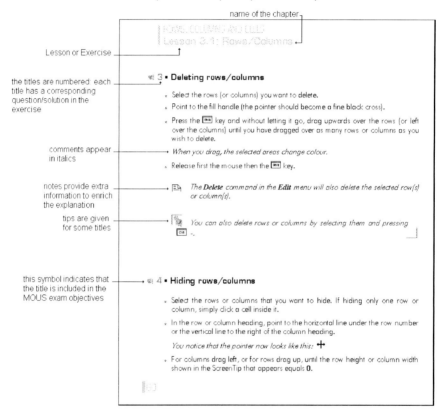

You can distinguish whether an action should be performed with the mouse, the keyboard or with the menu options by referring to the symbol that introduces each action: ⌐, ⊠ and ▤.

Installing the CD-ROM

The CD-ROM provided contains documents used in some of the practice exercises. When you follow the installation procedure set out below, a folder called MOUS Outlook 2000 is created on your hard disk and the CD-ROM documents are decompressed and copied into the created folder.

▪ Put the CD-ROM into the CD-ROM drive of your computer.

▪ Start the Windows Explorer: click the **Start** button, point to the **Programs** option then click **Windows Explorer**.

▪ In the left pane of the Explorer window, scroll through the list until the CD-ROM drive icon appears. Click this icon.

The contents of the CD-ROM appear in the right pane of the Explorer window. The documents you are going to be working on in the exercises appear in their compressed form MOUS Outlook 2000.exe, but you can also find them in the Summary and Practice Exercises folders.

▪ Double-click the icon of the **MOUS Outlook 2000** file in the right pane of the Explorer window.

*The **MOUS Outlook 2000** dialog box appears.*

▪ Click **Next**.

The installation application offers to create a folder called MOUS Outlook 2000.

▪ Modify the proposed folder name if you wish then click **Next**. If several people are going to be doing the practice exercises on the same computer, you should modify the folder name so each person is working on their own copy of the folder.

※ Click **Yes** to confirm creating the **MOUS Outlook 2000** folder.

The installation application decompresses the documents then copies them into the created folder.

※ Click **Finish** when the copying process is finished.

※ When the copy is finished, click the ☒ button on the **Explorer** window to close it.

You can now put away the CD-ROM and start working on your Microsoft Office User Specialist exam preparation.

OUTLOOK 2000
Lesson 1.1: Discovering the environment

1 ▪ Starting/leaving Outlook 2000

Microsoft Outlook lets you manage personal and professional information (such as e-mail messages, appointments, meetings and contacts), share information in a workgroup or with other programs and connect to the Internet and share information over the World Wide Web.

Starting Outlook

▪ Click the **Start** button on the taskbar.

▪ Choose the **Programs** menu and click the **Microsoft Outlook** option.

▪ If necessary, select the profile you want to use from the **Profile Name** drop-down list.

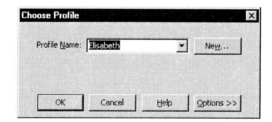

A user profile is a collection of parameters that defines your working configuration.

*You will be asked to choose your user profile if, in the **Options** dialog box (**Tools - Options - Mail Services** tab), the **Prompt for a profile to be used** option is active.*

▪ Click **OK**.

A screen showing the name of the program appears.

Now the Microsoft Outlook screen appears.

(a)   (b)   (c)

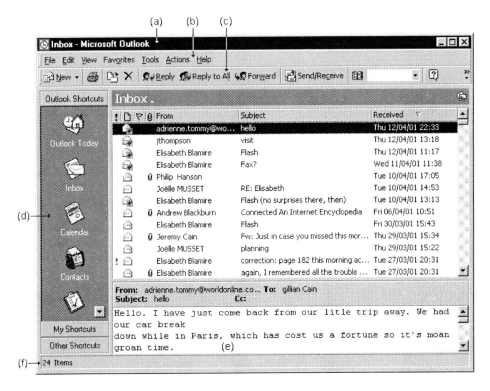

(d)

(e)

(f)

The screen you see when you open Outlook may differ slightly from the one shown here.

The **title bar** (a) contains Outlook's **System** menu icon (⬚) on the left, followed by the name of the selected folder (**Inbox, Calendar, Journal**, etc) followed by the name of the application (**Microsoft Outlook**).

On the right, the **Minimize** button (⬚) reduces the window to a button on the taskbar without closing the application; the **Restore** (⬚) button reduces the window so that it only uses part of the screen, in which case the **Restore** button is replaced by the **Maximize** (⬚) button which enlarges the window to fill the whole screen; finally, the **Close** (⬚) button closes the application.

The **menu bar** (b) contains the various menus available in Microsoft Outlook.

The **Standard** toolbar (c) contains tool buttons that will run some of the most common commands in the program. This bar's contents change depending on the active folder (**Inbox, Calendar, Contacts**…). You can show and hide it using **View - Toolbars - Standard**.

The **Outlook** bar (d) gives access to different groups (**Outlook Shortcuts, My Shortcuts, Other Shortcuts**). In each group are shortcuts to the folders which you will be using most often.

The **Preview Pane** (e) enables you to read an item (a message) without opening it. This pane does not appear in the **Outlook Today** folder.

The **status bar** (f) contains information about the current view. You can show and hide it using **View - Status Bar**.

It is possible that a shortcut for Outlook has been placed on the Windows Desktop. If this is the case, double-clicking the *icon will open the Outlook application.*

*Three further toolbars can be displayed using **View - Toolbars**: the **Remote, Advanced** and **Web** toolbars.*

Leaving Outlook

* To close Outlook but remain connected to the server, use **File - Exit**, click the ⊠ button on the Outlook window or press Alt F4.

* To close Outlook and disconnect from the server, use **File - Exit and Log Off**.

2 ▪ Accessing the different elements of Outlook

*The Outlook bar gives you access to different groups: **Outlook Shortcuts, My Shortcuts, Other Shortcuts**.*

* Use the **View - Outlook Bar** command to show and hide the Outlook bar (you can also right-click the Outlook bar and choose the **Hide Outlook Bar** option to hide the bar).

※ To see the contents of a group, click its name:

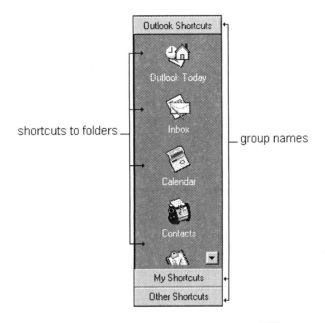

shortcuts to folders ⎯⎯⎯ [Outlook Shortcuts / Outlook Today / Inbox / Calendar / Contacts / My Shortcuts / Other Shortcuts] ⎯⎯ group names

※ If you cannot see all the active group, click the [▼] or [▲] buttons to scroll the group's contents.

※ The **Outlook Shortcuts** group contains the following folders:

Outlook Today	contains a view of the day: your calendar, your task list and the status of your messages.
Inbox	contains the messages you have received.
Calendar	contains your appointments, events and meetings.
Contacts	contains a list of the names and addresses of the people you communicate with.
Tasks	contains all the tasks you have, which you can follow until their completion.

Notes	contains a list a notes you have written for yourself or for others.
Deleted Items	contains all the items you have deleted from other folders.

* The **My Shortcuts** group contains the following folders:

Drafts	use this folder to store saved messages which you can then send later.
Outbox	contains all the messages waiting to be sent.
Sent Items	contains a copy of all sent messages, provided that the **Save copies of messages in Sent Items folder** option is active in the **E-mail Options** dialog box (**Tools - Options**, **Preferences** tab, **E-mail Options** button).
Journal	contains your Journal entries, which represent a timeline of your activities (messages, meetings, Microsoft Office documents, etc).
Outlook Update	contains a shortcut to Microsoft's Outlook page.

* The **Other Shortcuts** group contains folders that enable you to access your documents: **My Computer**, the **My Documents** folder and the **Favorites** folder (which can display the Web pages you view most often).

 *Drag the righthand border of the Outlook bar to increase or decrease its width. To display the items in each group as large or small icons, activate the group in question, right-click the Outlook bar and choose **Large Icons** or **Small Icons**.*

*Use the **View - Go To** command to go into a different folder without using the Outlook bar.*

Mags

m.mckeogh @ ntlworld.com.

Maggie60.

3 ▪ Displaying the folder list and the preview pane

The **Folder List** shows the hierarchy of Outlook's folders. It can be very useful when the Outlook bar is hidden and also gives access to public folders.

▫ Display the folder list temporarily by clicking the title of the current folder:

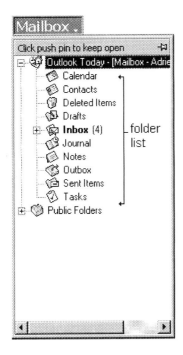

folder
list

You can change the width of the folder list by dragging its righthand border.

▫ To display the folder list permanently, use **View - Folder List** or click the tool button (**Advanced** toolbar) or click the icon that appears when you click the folder's title.

Outllook lists all the folders it can find. The folders preceded by a plus sign contain subfolders.

When a folder's name is followed by a number in brackets, this number indicates the number of unread items the folder contains.

* Click the + sign to see the subfolders of a folder.

* To see a folder's contents, click its name.

If the folder list is displayed temporarily, it disappears as soon as you click a folder name and the name of the active folder changes.

* To close the folder list, click the ☒ button you can see in the top right of the folder list window or use **View - Folder List**.

* To display (or hide) the preview pane, use **View - Preview Pane** or 🗒 (**Advanced** toolbar).

The contents of the message which is currently selected appears in the preview pane.

4 ▪ Using the help

Using the help without the Office Assistant

* Make sure the Office Assistant is deactivated. To do this, show the Office Assistant using **Help - Show Office Assistant** then right-click the Assistant and choose **Options**. Deactivate the **Use the Office Assistant** option and click **OK**.

* **Help - Microsoft Outlook Help** or F1

❋ To search for a topic in the table of contents, click the **Contents** tab, click a book to open a category then click the question mark for the topic you want:

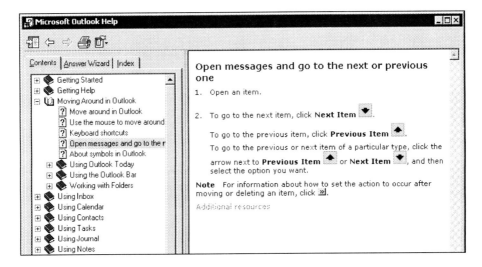

*The help for the topic appears in the right pane of the **Microsoft Outlook Help** window.*

❋ To see the topics that correspond to a question, click the **Answer Wizard** tab and type your question in the **What would you like to do?** box, click the **Search** button then select the appropriate help topic.

❋ To search for a topic using the index, click the **Index** tab then type the first words of the topic in the **Type keywords** text box or double-click one of the words in the **Or choose keywords** list. Select the help topic you want to display in the righthand pane.

❋ You can hide the **Contents**, **Answer Wizard** and **Index** tabs by clicking the ⌷. Click ⌷ to show them again.

❋ Click the ⌷ button to show the preceding help topic.

❋ To show the next help topic, click ⌷.

* Click the 🖨 tool button to print the active help topic, define the printing options in the **Print** dialog box then click **OK**. If you found the topic via the **Contents** tab, a message appears offering to **Print the selected topic** or **Print the selected heading and all subtopics**. If this happens, click the appropriate option then click **OK**.

* Once you have finished using the help, click the ☒ button.

Using the help with the Office Assistant

* If necessary, show the Office Assistant using **Help - Show Office Assisant**.

  If the Office Assistant has not been deactivated but is hidden, click the 🔲 tool button or use **Help - Microsoft Outlook Help** or press 🔳 to show it.

* Click the Assisant to open the **What would you like to do?** window.

* Click one of the subjects suggested by the Assistant to see the corresponding help topic or type a keyword in the text box and click the **Search** button.

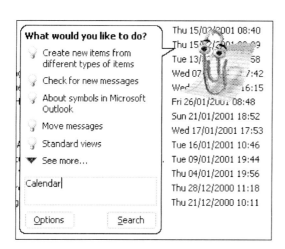

The help topics corresponding to your keyword appear. Use the **See more** option to show the rest of the topics found.

* Click the appropriate topic to see the help.

* Read the help then, if necessary, click the ⊞ tool button to show the **Contents**, **Answer Wizard** and **Index** tabs so that you can make a new search in the **Microsoft Outlook Help** window (see the subheading above).

* When you have finished in the **Microsoft Outlook Help** window, click the ☒ button to close it.

* If you want to change the appearance of the Office Assistant, right-click the Assistant and click **Choose Assistant**. Use the **Next** and/or **Back** buttons to find the Assistant you want then click **OK**. If necessary, insert the Microsoft Office 2000 CD-ROM into the drive and click **Yes** to the message asking if you want to install the chosen Assistant.

* Hide the Office Assistant using **Help - Hide Office Assistant** or right-click the Assistant and choose **Hide**.

* To deactivate the Office Assistant use **Help - Microsoft Office Help** if it is hidden or click the Assistant if it is visible. Click the **Options** button, deactivate the **Use Office Assistant** option then click **OK**.

*Use **Help - Show Office Assistant** to reactivate the Assistant.*

 When the Assistant is hidden (but not deactivated) it may reappear when it has a tip for you (in which case, it appears accompanied by a lightbulb); click the Assistant to see the tip.

*If the Assistant cannot help you with your problem, you can search for help on the Internet using the **Microsoft Office on the Web** command in the **Help** menu.*

Below you can see **Practice exercise 1.1**. This exercise is made up of 4 steps. If you do not know how to complete one of the steps, go back to the lesson to refer to the corresponding title. When you have finished, check your work by reading the **Solution** on the next page.

Steps that are likely to be tested on the exam are marked with a ▦ symbol. It is however recommended that you follow the whole exercice in order to gain a complete understanding of the lesson.

☞ **Practice exercise 1.1**

    1. Start Microsoft Office and discover the Outlook screen.

▦ 2. Show the contents of the **Sent Items** folder then the **Outlook Today** folder.

    3. Show the folder list temporarily then select the **Inbox** folder.
Display the preview pane in the **Sent Items** folder then return to the **Inbox** folder.

▦ 4. Display the Office Assistant then show the help for writing a message. Close the help window and hide the Assistant.

If you want to put what you have learned into practice in a real document, you can work on the summary exercise 1 for the OUTLOOK 2000 section that you can find at the end of this book.

It is often possible to perform a task in several different ways, but here only the quickest solution is presented. Go back to the lesson to see the other techniques that can be used.

 Solution to exercise 1.1

1. Start Microsoft Outllook 2000 by clicking the **Start** button on the the task bar, click the **Programs** menu and choose **Microsoft Outlook**.

2. To display the contents of the Sent Items folder, open the **My Shortcuts** group in the **Outlook** bar then click the **Sent Items** folder. Show the contents of the Outlook Today folder by showing the **Outlook Shortcuts** group (click the corresponding button on the **Outlook** bar), then clicking the **Outlook Today** folder.

3. Display the folder list temporarily and select the Inbox folder by clicking the title of the **Outlook Today** folder (for example, **Mailbox - Claire Wilson - Outlook Today**) then click **Inbox**.

   To show the preview pane in the Sent Items folder, open the **My Shortcuts** group in the **Outlook** bar. Click the **Sent Items** folder to display its contents then use **View - Preview Pane**. To show the Inbox folder again, choose **Outlook Shortcuts** in the **Outlook** bar and click the **Inbox** shortcut.

4. Use **Help - Show Office Assistant** to display the Office Assistant.
   To show the help for writing messages, click the Assistant, type **writing messages** in the text box and click **Search**. Click **Create a message**. If necessary, click the ⬜ button to increase the size of the **Microsoft Outlook Help** window then, having read the help, close the window by clicking ⬜. Hide the Office Assistant by right-clicking it and choosing **Hide**.

E-MAIL
Lesson 2.1: Sending a message

1 ▪ What is electronic mail?

- Electronic mail is a means of sending and receiving messages electronically, via your computer.

- There are four folders that can contain messages:
  - the **Inbox** folder in the **Outlook Shortcuts** group.
  - the **Drafts**, **Outbox** and **Sent Items** folders in the **My Shortcuts** group.

- Access these folders by clicking the name of the group they are in then clicking the folder's name.

2 ▪ Creating and sending a message

- There are three techniques for creating a new message:
  - **File - New - Mail Message** or **Ctrl** **N**

  - **Actions - New Mail Message** or **Ctrl** **N**

  - Select a message folder (**Inbox**, **Sent Items**, etc) and click the **New ▾** button on the **Standard** toolbar.

  The message window appears on the screen.

- Enter the address of the message recipient in the **To** box using one of the two methods below:

  - Type the address(es), separating them with a comma or semi-colon.

  *You can type an Internet e-mail address in the **To** box (cbrown@eni.com)*
  or

  you can click the *button to select addresses from an address book (providing you have entered addresses into your address book).*

  *The **Select Names** dialog box appears and you can see addresses for your correspondents.*

If you have more than one address book, open the **Show Names from the** list and choose the appropriate address book.

For each addressee, select their name in the **Type Name or Select from List** boxes and click the ▭ To -> button, or double-click the name. To select several people at once, use the ▭ Shift key to select adjacent names or the ▭ Ctrl key for non-adjacent names.

*If you want to go to a name in the list quickly, type the first letters of the name in the **Type Name or Select from List** text box.*

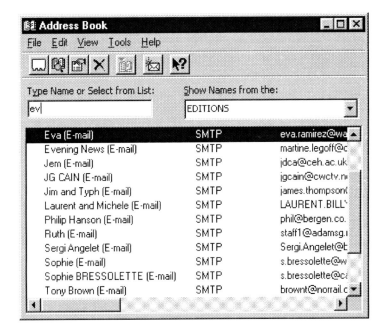

You can remove an addressee by selecting his/her name in the **Message Recipients** list to the right of the ▭ To -> button then pressing ▭ Del on the keyboard.

Click **OK**.

*When you leave the **To** field, the address of the recipient is underlined if it is recognised by Outlook, provided the **Automatic name checking** option in the **Advanced E-mail Options** dialog box is active (in the main Outlook window, use **Tools - Options - Preferences** tab, click the **E-mail Options** button then the **Advanced E-mail Options** button).*

※ In the **Cc** (carbon copy) box, type the address(es) of any correspondents who are to receive a copy of the message or click the **Cc** button to select addresses from an address book in the same way as you would for the **To** box.

Copies of messages are sent for information only and assume that you do not expect a reply from these recipients.

※ If you want to send a copy of the message to hidden recipients, show the **Bcc** box (Blind carbon copy) using **View - Bcc Field** then click the ⬚ Bcc... button to select addresses from an address book.

*The recipients in the **To** and **Cc** boxes will not know that the people in the **Bcc** box have received the message.*

※ In the **Subject** field, type the subject of your message.

The subject is seen by the message recipient and can influence his or her decision to read your message.

※ Use the large text box to type the message body text and, if necessary, change the formatting of the text.

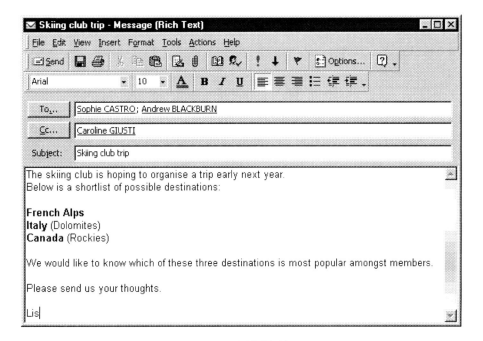

* Send the message using **File - Send** or [⧉ Send] or [Ctrl] [↵].

  *The message window disappears. If the message is sent successfully, a copy of it is stored in the **Sent Items** folder (assuming the **Save copies of messages in Sent Items folder** option is active in the **E-mail Options** dialog box (**Tools - Options - Preferences** tab - **E-mail Options** button). The message appears in each recipient's Inbox preceded by the unread message symbol: ✉. If the message cannot be sent, it is kept in the **Outbox** folder.*

* If you do not want to send the message straight away, save it for later using

  File - Save or [💾] or [Ctrl] **S**

  *The message is stored in the **Drafts** folder in the **My Shortcuts** group and is preceded by this symbol: 📇.*

* To complete and/or send a message in the **Drafts** folder, activate this folder, open the message draft by double-clicking it, finish the message or make any required changes and click the 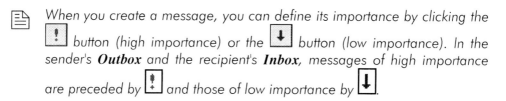 button.

*The message disappears from the **Drafts** folder.*

When you create a message, you can define its importance by clicking the 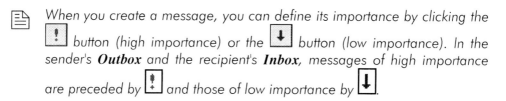 *button (high importance) or the* 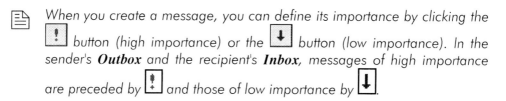 *button (low importance). In the sender's **Outbox** and the recipient's **Inbox**, messages of high importance are preceded by* 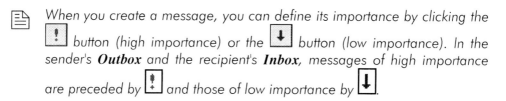 *and those of low importance by* 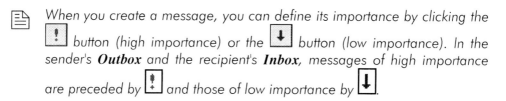.

If you try to close a message you have not saved, Outlook asks if you want to save it.

3 ▪ Managing message text

Checking the spelling in a message

* You need to be creating or editing a message.

* If you want to check all the text, place the insertion point at the beginning of the big text box. If you only want to check part of the message, select this text by dragging.

* **Tools - Spelling** or F7

*As soon as a misspelled word is found, Outlook shows it in the **Not in Dictionary** box.*

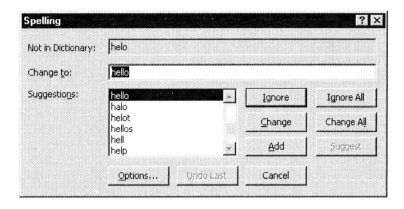

* Depending on the case, use one of the following buttons:

Ignore To leave the word in the **Not in Dictionary** box unchanged and continue checking.

Ignore All To leave every occurrence of the word in the **Not in Dictionary** box unchanged and continue checking.

Add To add the word in the **Not in Dictionary** box to the dictionary so that Outlook will recognise it from now on.

Change To replace the word in the **Not in Dictionary** box by the word in the **Change To** box. You can also double-click one of the **Suggestions** in the corresponding list.

Change All To replace all occurrences of the word with the word in the **Change To** box. Again, you could double-click one of the **Suggestions**.

Undo Last To undo the last action carried out in the spelling check.

Delete/Delete All Appears when a word is repeated and can be used to delete it.

* When you have finished the spelling check a message appears: click **OK**.

Formatting characters

You can change the way characters look by applying bold type, italics or underlining, for example.

※ You need to be creating or editing a message.

※ If necessary, display the **Formatting** toolbar. Do this using **View - Toolbars** and the **Formatting** option (when a toolbar is active, a tick appears next to its name).

*You can also right-click a toolbar and choose **Formatting**.*

※ If the text has been typed, select it.

※ Use the tools on the **Formatting** toolbar:

Arial	to apply the **Font**.
10	to change the **Size**.
A	to change the **Color** of the text.
B	to apply or remove **Bold** formatting.
I	to apply or remove an **Italic** style.
U	to apply or remove the **Underline** style.

📄 *You can also use the options in the **Font** dialog box (**Format - Font**) to format your text.*

🔍 *If you want to remove all the formatting from the selected characters at once, press* 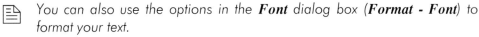 Ctrl Space.

Formatting paragraphs

Each paragraph is ended with a carriage return (obtained by pressing ⤶).

- You need to be creating or editing a message.
- If need be, display the **Formatting** toolbar by using **View - Toolbars** and choosing **Formatting**.
- Click in the paragraph in question or select the paragraphs.
- Use these tools on the **Formatting** toolbar:

    to align text on the left.

    to centre the text.

    to align text on the right.

    to insert or remove a bullet from in front of the paragraph.

    to decrease the paragraph's left indent.

    to increase the paragraph's left indent.

 *The options for aligning text and inserting bullets are available in the **Paragraph** dialog box (**Format - Paragraph**).*

If you use Word as your e-mail editor (see Creating a message using an Office application), it opens whenever you create a new message and you can use all its formatting options (borders, tables, numbered lists, hanging indents and so on).

⊞4 ▪ **Creating a message using stationery**

Outlook provides a selection of predefined stationery designs to liven up your message backgrounds.

▪ Select one of the message folders.

▪ **Actions - New Mail Message Using - More Stationery**

▪ Select the **Stationery** you want to use from the list:

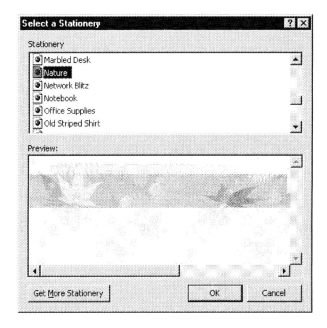

*You can click each option to see a **Preview** in the corresponding box.*

*It is possible that some of the stationery in the list is not installed on your computer. If this is the case, Outlook will ask if you want to install it after you validate the **Select a Stationery** dialog box.*

▪ Click **OK**.

* If you have selected stationery that is not installed on your computer, click **Yes** to the message asking if you want to install it now, insert the Microsoft Office 2000 CD-ROM then click **OK**.

The message creation window appears and the chosen stationery appears in the background of the message body.

* Continue the message as you would any message (see Creating and sending a message).

* If necessary, make changes to the stationery using the **Formatting** toolbar.

* Click the ⌐Send button to send the message.

 *To create a message using stationery you have already used, choose **Actions - New Mail Message Using** and click the name of the stationery you want from the list above **More Stationery**.*

5 • Templates

If you regularly send the same type of message to people, you can save the message's skeleton (all the unchanging information) as a template so that you do not have to recreate the message each time you want to send it.

Creating a message template

* **File - New - Mail Message** or New ▾ or Ctrl **N**

* Enter the information you want to re-use for each message.

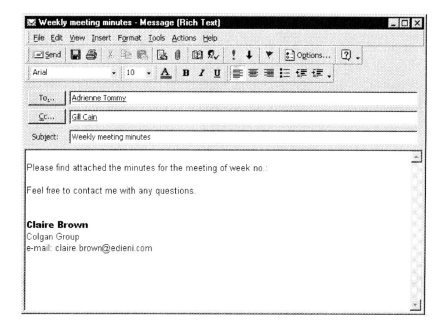

Before sending this message, the user will only have to enter the appropriate week number for the meeting and insert the minutes as an attachment.

※ **File - Save As**

※ Type the template's name in the **File name** box.

※ Open the **Save as type** list and select **Outlook Template (*.oft)**.

*The **C:\WINDOWS\Application Data\Microsoft\Templates** folder is selected automatically. In Outlook, message templates carry the extension **oft**.*

※ Click **Save**.

※ Click the ☒ button to close the message.

A message appears.

※ Click **Yes** if you want to save the message in the **Drafts** folder; if not, click **No**.

Creating a new message from a template

- **File - New - Choose Form**
- Open the **Look In** list and choose **User Templates in File System**.

  *A list of the templates in the **Templates** folder appears.*

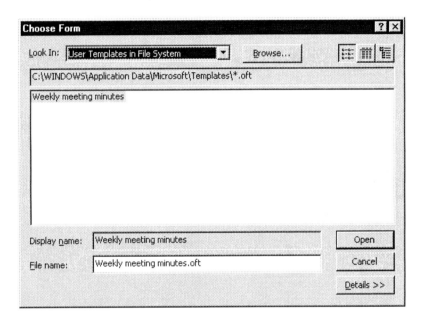

*The path to the folder that contains the templates is shown under the **Look In** list.*

- Select the template you want to use and click **Open**.

  You can also double-click a template to open it.

- If need be, complete the message with any variable information.
- Send the message: **File - Send** or [≡ Send].

⊞6 ▪ Inserting a signature

Creating signatures

You can create several signatures to customise your messages.

* In the main Outlook window use **Tools - Options** and click the **Mail Format** tab.

* Make sure the **Use Microsoft Word to edit e-mail messages** option is not active. If you want to use signatures, you cannot use Word as your default editor.

* Click the **Signature Picker** button then the **New** button.

* **Enter a name for your new signature** in the corresponding text box.

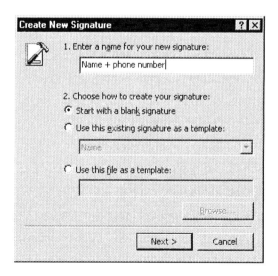

* Indicate how you want to create your signature:

  - **Start with a blank signature** to create everything in your signature.

  - **Use this existing signature as a template**; open the associated list and choose the signature that is to be the base for the new one. This option is not available if this is the first time you have created a signature.

- **Use this file as a template**; enter the file path and the file name or click **Browse** to select the file.

⊛ Click **Next**.

⊛ Type or edit the text of the signature in the first text box and apply formatting using the **Font** and **Paragraph** buttons.

⊛ If you have electronic business cards and you want to add one to the end of the signature, open the **Attach this business card (vCard) to this signature** list and choose the card you want to use.

*The **New vCard from Contact** button enables you to create a new business card from your address book.*

⊛ Click **Finish**.

*In the **Preview** frame you can see the text of the selected signature.*

⊛ Click **OK** to validate the **Signature Picker** dialog box.

*The **Options** dialog box reappears on screen. You will notice that the last signature you created is visible in the list next to **Use this Signature by default**.*

⊛ If you do not want to use this last signature by default, open the **Use this Signature by default** list and choose **None>**.

⊛ Click **OK** to validate the **Options** dialog box.

 *To edit or delete a signature, open the **Signature Picker** dialog box (**Tools - Options, Mail Format** tab, **Signature Picker** button), select the signature in question and use the **Edit** or **Remove** button.*

Inserting a signature into a message

To do this you will need to have created a signature (see previous subheading).

⊛ You need to be creating or editing a message.

⊛ Place the insertion point where you want to insert the signature.

❋ **Insert - Signature** or [image]

❋ Click the name of the signature you want to insert.

*If you use the menu command, the **More** option opens the **Signature Picker** dialog box.*

Signing messages automatically

You can choose an automatic signature so that you do not have to insert one into each message.

❋ In the main Outlook window, use **Tools - Options** and click the **Mail Format** tab.

❋ In the **Use this Signature by default** list, select the name of the signature you want to insert in all your messages.

❋ If you do not want to insert your signature when you reply to or forward messages, activate the **Don't use when replying or forwarding** option.

❋ Click **OK**.

▦7 ▪ Inserting an attachment

This technique involves attaching a document to a message.

❋ While you are creating or editing a message, place the insertion point where you want to insert the document.

❋ **Insert - File** or [image]

❋ Select the drive where the document is stored using the **Look In** list.

❋ Go to the folder that contains the document by double-clicking the yellow folder icon.

❋ Select the name of the document you want to insert in the message.

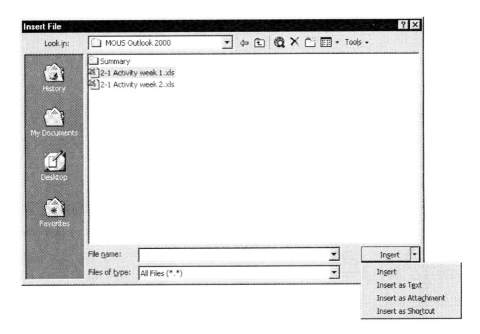

» Click the **Insert** button or open the list on this button and choose:

Insert as Text to insert the document as text in the message body (the text must not contain any presentation items).

Insert as Attachment to insert the document as an attachment.

Insert as Shortcut to insert a shortcut to the document. Use this option if the document you are inserting is very big.

*Clicking the **Insert** button is the same as choosing **Insert as Attachment**.*

If you have chosen the second or third option, the document appears as an icon:

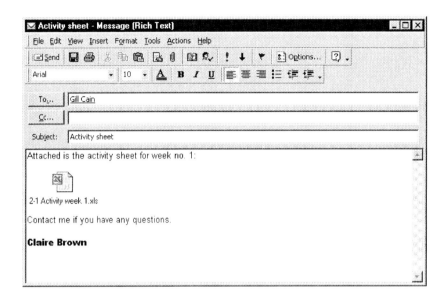

* Click [Send] to send the message.

📄 *The sender and recipient see messages with an attachment preceded by this symbol:* 📎.

📖 8 ▪ Inserting an Outlook item into a message

* You need to be creating or editing a message.
* Place the insertion point where the Outlook item should be inserted.
* **Insert - Item**

   The ***Insert Item*** window appears.
* Use the **Look in** list to select the folder that contains the item in question.

» In the **Items** list, select the item(s) you want to insert. To select several items, use the `Shift` key for adjacent items and/or the `Ctrl` key for non-adjacent items.

» Choose how you want to insert the item in the **Insert as** frame:

Text only   to insert the item as text in the message body.

Attachment   to insert the item as an attachment.

Shortcut   to insert a shortcut to the item.

» Click **OK**.

*Outlook items that have been inserted as **Attachments** or **Shortcuts** appear in messages as icons that indicate their origin:*

Gina Bazeley   Access   Check that the MSCE
                                          files have...

Team meeting   Send invitations

9 ▪ Creating a message using an Office application

*You can create a message whose content is created using the **Microsoft Word** word processor, the **Microsoft Excel** spreadsheet, the **Microsoft PowerPoint** computer-assisted presentation package or the **Microsoft Access** database management system. Obviously, these applications need to be installed on your computer, but your correspondents will be able to read the message even if they do not have the relevant applications on their computers.*

» Select one of the message folders or **Outlook Today**.

» **Actions - New Mail Message Using - Microsoft Office**

* Choose to create a message using a **Microsoft Word Document**, a **Microsoft PowerPoint Slide**, a **Microsoft Excel Worksheet** or a **Microsoft Access Data Page**.

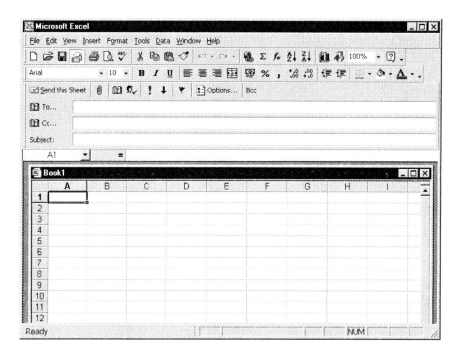

*The corresponding application opens. Its **Standard** toolbar appears as well as the **To, Cc** and **Subject** boxes from **Outlook**. The illustration above shows a message that will be created using Microsoft Excel.*

* Enter the addresses or select them using the **To** and **Cc** buttons in the same way as you would for any message.

* Enter the **Subject** of the message in the appropriate text box.

* Create the message body using the features of the active application.

* Click the **Send** button: the label on the **Send** button changes according to the application in use (**Send a Copy** for Word and Access, **Send this Sheet** for Excel and **Send this Slide** for PowerPoint).

- If necessary, save the contents of the message as a file from the active application. Do this with **File - Save** (or ▣ or Ctrl **S**), select the drive and folder where you want to save the file, give the **File name** in the relevant box and click **Save**.

- Close the application by clicking ☒. If you do not want to save the message contents as a file in the application, click **No** in the message asking if you want to save the changes.

- If need be, reactivate Outlook by clicking its button on the task bar.

 *You can choose to use Word as your default message editor. Do this by activating the **Use Microsoft Word to edit e-mail messages** option in the **Options** dialog box (**Tools - Options - Mail Format** tab). Once you do this, Word will open each time you create a new message and you can use all its formatting tools (borders, tables, numbered lists, hanging indents and so on) in your messages.*

10 ▪ Selecting addresses from an address book

To make entering addresses easier and to eliminate the risk of typing errors, you can use address books.

- While you are creating or editing a message, use the **To** and **Cc** buttons to select addresses from an address book.

  The **Select Names** dialog box appears.

- If you are using more than one address book, use the **Show Names from the** list to select the appropriate address book.

- For each address you want to add:

  - Select it from those shown under **Type Name or Select from List**. To select several addresses at once, use the Shift key for adjacent names and the Ctrl key for non-adjacent names.

- Click the [To ->], [Cc ->] or [Bcc...] buttons, depending on where you want to insert the address.

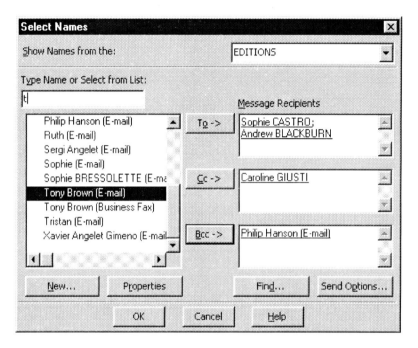

You can also double-click a name to add it to the active box.

⁜ Remove an address by clicking the name in one of the boxes (**To**, **Cc** or **Bcc**) in the **Message Recipients** column (one click is enough to select a name) and press [Del].

⁜ Click **OK**.

⁜ Carry on creating or editing the message.

⁜ Click the [≡ Send] button to send the message.

📄 *You can select contacts from different address books.*

▦11 ▪ Flagging a message for follow up

You can place a follow up flag on a message to remind you that the message requires further action (indicated by the accompanying text).

Adding a follow up flag to a message

▪ While you are creating or editing a message, use **Actions - Flag for Follow Up** or [▼] or [Ctrl] [Shift] **G**.

▪ Open the **Flag to** list to choose the text that will accompany the follow up flag.

▪ If necessary, open the **Due by** list to choose a due date or type the date directly into the corresponding text box.

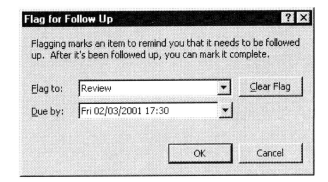

▪ Click **OK**.

▪ Finish the message if need be then click the [≡]Send button.

*Messages that have a flag are shown with a [▼] symbol in the sender's **Sent Items** folder and the recipients' **Inbox**.*

The message recipient(s) can see the text for the follow up action when the message is opened.

The **View - Current View - By Follow-up Flag** command lets you display only messages that have a follows up flag. You can choose to show only messages with a flag whose due date is in the next seven days using **View - Current View - Flagged for Next Seven Days**.

Adding a completed flag

The message recipient should add a completed flag once the follow up task is achieved.

※ Select a message that has a follow up flag.

※ **Actions - Flag for Follow Up** or [▼] or ⌈Ctrl⌉⌈Shift⌉ **G**

※ Activate the **Completed** option.

※ Click **OK**.

Messages that are completed are shown with this symbol: [▽].

Removing a follow-up flag

※ Select a message that has a follow up flag.

※ **Actions - Flag for Follow Up** or [▼] or ⌈Ctrl⌉⌈Shift⌉ **G**

※ Click **Clear Flag**.

🔍 *You can also add a flag to an existing message (or clear a flag) by right-clicking the message and choosing the **Flag for Follow Up** option.*

▦12 ▪ Resending a message

If your correspondent is taking time to reply to your message or you need to change a message you have sent, you can resend it.

▪ In the **Outlook** bar, select the **My Shortcuts** group and click **Sent Items**.

▪ Open the message you want to resend by double-clicking it.

In the window that appears, the 📧Send *button is missing.*

▪ **Actions - Resend This Message**

▪ If need be, change the message contents.

▪ Resend the message by clicking 📧Send .

▪ Close the old message window by clicking ☒ or by **File - Close**.

*The message you have resent is added to the items in the **Sent Items** folder.*

▦13 ▪ Recalling/replacing a message that has been sent

In Outlook you have the possibility or recalling or replacing a message that you have sent. However, the message must not have been read by the recipients. This feature is only available if you are working with Microsoft Exchange Server.

▪ Select the **My Shortcuts** group on the **Outlook** bar and click the **Sent Items** folder.

▪ Open the message in question with a double-click.

▪ **Actions - Recall This Message**

* To recall the message, activate the **Delete unread copies of this message** option. Choose **Delete unread copies and replace with a new message** if you want to replace the message.

* If you want to know the result of the recall, activate the **Tell me if recall succeeds or fails for each recipient** option.

* Click **OK**.

* If you have chosen to replace the message, make the necessary changes and click [Send].

* Close the message window by clicking [X].

    When the recall is successful, the message disappears from the recipients' Inboxes and appears in the sender's Inbox with this message:

    Gillian CAIN   Message Recall Success: Thursday's meeting   Tue 17/04/01 16:47

If the recall is not successful, the following message appears in the sender's Inbox:

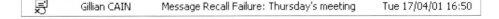

    Gillian CAIN   Message Recall Failure: Thursday's meeting   Tue 17/04/01 16:50

14 ▪ Sending a voting message

You can send a message whose reply involves voting. The recipient casts his or her vote by clicking voting buttons. This feature is only available if you are working with Microsoft Exchange Server.

▪ While you are creating or editing a message, use **View - Options** or click the ⌷ Options... button.

▪ Activate the **Use voting buttons** option.

▪ Open the **Use voting buttons** list and choose the voting buttons you want to use. You can also create your own voting buttons. To do this, select the contents of the **Use voting buttons** text box and delete them before typing the text for your own buttons, using a semi-colon to separate them.

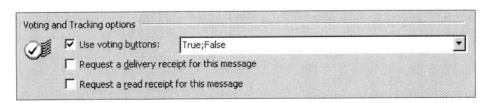

▪ Click **Close**.

▪ Continue your message and send it by clicking ⌷ Send .

📄 *The voting buttons appear when the recipient opens the message, allowing him or her to reply by casting a vote.*

. *Once the recipients have voted, the replies precede the message subject in the sender's Inbox. You can also see the replies by opening the voting message in the Sent Items folder and clicking the **Tracking** tab.*

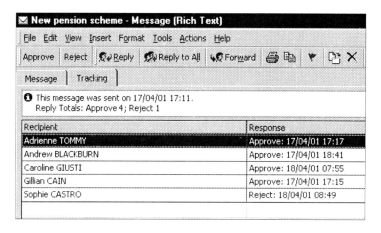

15 • Defining a message's tracking options

⁕ While you are creating or editing a message, use **View - Options** or click the
📄 Options... button.

⁕ If you want another user to receive the replies, type their name or e-mail address in the **Have replies sent to** text box or click the **Select Names** button to choose the name from an address book.

⁕ If you want to know when the recipients have received the message, activate the **Request a delivery receipt for this message** option. You will receive a message telling you the date and time the recipient(s) received the message.

⁕ If you want to know when the recipients have read the message, activate **Request a read receipt for this message** to receive an automatic conformation message telling you the date and time the recipient(s) read the message.

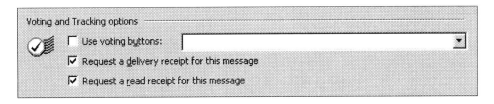

* Click **Close**.

* Finish the message if need be and click 🖃 Send .

*In the sender's **Inbox** the subject of a received message is preceded by the text **Delivered** and that of a read message by **Read**.*

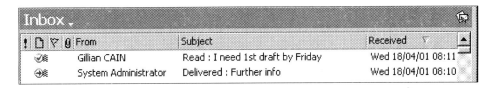

*When you open a message in which you have activated the **Request a delivery receipt for this message** and/or **Request a read receipt for this message** option, the window has an extra tab: **Tracking**. In this tab you can see a list of the recipients and information about when they received the message. The system will take a moment or two to display the contents of the tab.*

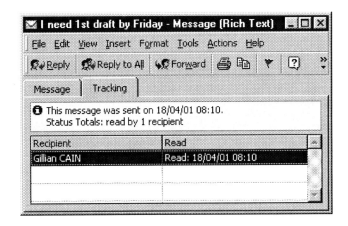

If you want the system to track your messages automatically, open the **Tracking Options** *dialog box (***Tools - Options***,* **Preferences** *tab,* **E-mail Options** *and* **Tracking Options** *buttons) and activate the* **Request a read receipt for all messages I send** *and/or* **Request a delivery receipt for all messages I send** *options.*

16 ▪ Sending an automatic reply whilst absent

You can choose to send an automatic reply to users who send you messages while you are absent. This feature is only available with Microsoft Exchange Server.

⊛ Activate one of the message folders.

⊛ **Tools - Out of Office Assistant**

⊛ Activate the **I am currently Out of the Office** option.

⊛ Complete the **AutoReply only once to each sender with the following text** box.

⊛ Click **OK**.

When somebody sends you a message or invites you to a meeting during your absence they receive a message in their **Inbox** *whose subject is preceded by the words* **Out of Office AutoReply***.*

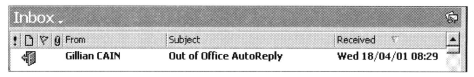

⊛ Indicate you are back by activating the **I am currently In the Office** option in the **Out of Office Assistant** dialog box (**Tools - Out of Office Assistant**).

This will not remove the messages sent to other users during your absence.

 If you close Outlook while the Out of Office Assistant is active, the next time you open Outlook a message asks you if you want to deactivate the Out of Office Assistant and indicate you are back.

Below you can see **Practice exercise 2.1**. This exercise is made up of 16 steps. If you do not know how to complete one of the steps, go back to the lesson to refer to the corresponding title. When you have finished, check your work by reading the **Solution** on the next page.

Steps that are likely to be tested on the exam are marked with a 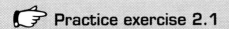 symbol. It is however recommended that you follow the whole exercice in order to gain a complete understanding of the lesson.

☞ **Practice exercise 2.1**

1. Display the contents of the **Sent Items** folder then the **Deleted Items** folder. Now return to the **Inbox**.

2. Create two messages according to the instructions below:

   - The first message is to be sent immediately to the recipient or your choice (two recipients in the **To** box and one of the **Cc** box) and should contain the following:

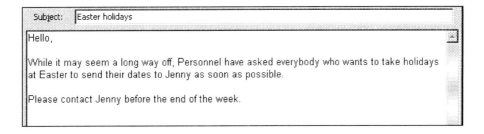

- The second message is to be saved so that you can edit it later before sending it to the recipients of your choice (two in the **To** box) and should contain the following information:

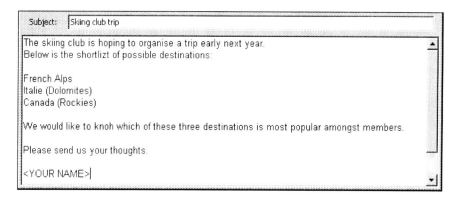

The spelling mistakes you can see are deliberate and you should make them too.

For both these messages, do not select the addresses from an address book but type them into each address field. If you cannot remember any e-mail addresses, you can always send the messages to yourself.

3. Check the spelling of the **Skiing trip** message in the **Drafts** folder. Make the formatting changes shown below so that the result resembles the one in the illustration then send the message:

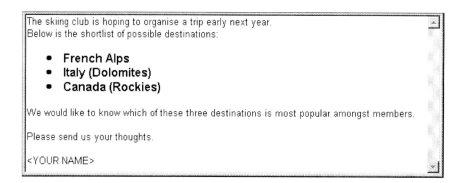

- Apply **Bold** type and font size **12** to **French Alps, Italy (Dolomites)** and **Canada (Rockies)**.

- Insert a bullet before the three paragraphs containing **French Alps, Italy (Dolomites)** and **Canada (Rockies)** and increase the left indent of these paragraphs once.

4. Create a message containing the information in the screen below using one of the predefined stationery designs and send the message to the recipient(s) or your choice (one or more names in the **To** box):

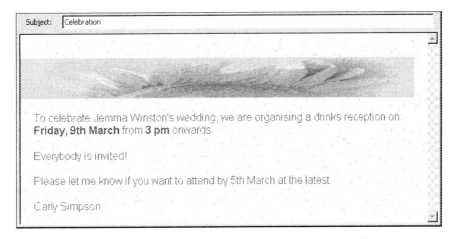

If you cannot remember any e-mail addresses, send the message to yourself.

5. Create a message template and call it **Activity sheet**. The template should contain the information shown below:

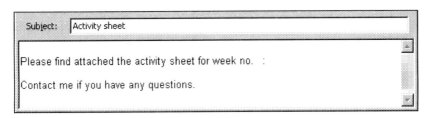

You can enter an address in the **To** box to define the recipient of all the messages based on the template. This could be your own address. Save the **Activity sheet** template in the **Templates** folder proposed by default.

When you have saved the template, close the message without saving it.

Now create a new message using the **Activity sheet** template you have just saved and make the following changes before sending it:

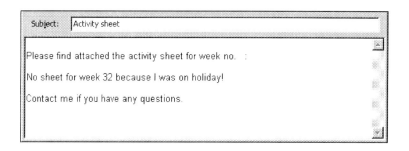

▦ 6. Create two signatures according to the following indications:

- **Name Surname** (apply Bold styling). Call this signature **Short**.

- **Name Surname** (apply Bold styling)

Tel.: 1234 567 0000 (your telephone number)

e-mail: (your e-mail address)

Call this signature **Long**.

Neither of these signatures should be the default signature. Now create a new message using the **Activity sheet** template and insert the **Short** signature after **Contact me if you have any questions**. Do not send this message.

▦ 7. Insert **2-1 Activity week 1.xls** from the **MOUS Outlook 2000** folder as an attachment after **Contact me if you have any questions** in the active message (the one you have just created but not sent) and send the message.

8. Create a new message as shown below:

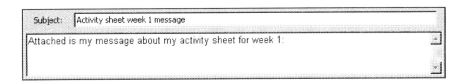

Now, after the message text, insert the Outlook item that corresponds to your last message (with an attachment and **Activity sheet** as the subject) as an attachment. Send the message with your choice of recipient in the **To** box.

You can always send the message to yourself if you cannot remember any e-mail addresses.

9. Create the message below using **Microsoft Word** and send it to the recipient of your choice (one name in the **To** box):

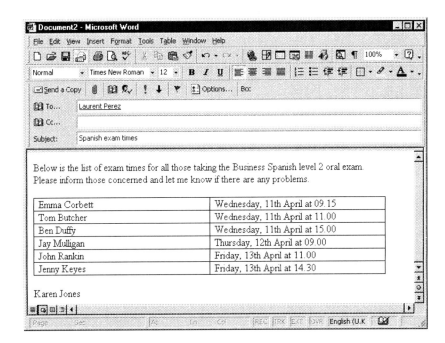

E-MAIL
Exercise 2.1: Sending a message

Finish by closing Microsoft Word without saving the message contents as a Word file.

You can always send the message to yourself if you cannot remember any e-mail addresses.

10. Create the message below and select the recipients' names from an address book (two or more names in the **To** box and one in the **Cc** box):

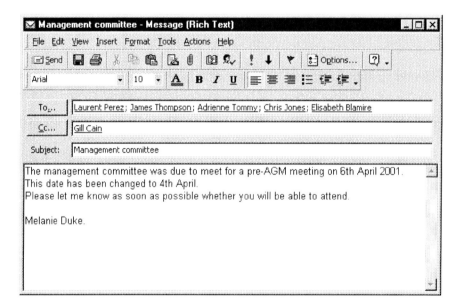

Do not send this message.

11. Add a follow up flag to the active message to tell the recipients that you expect a reply in no later than 7 day's time then send the message.

▣12. Make the changes shown below to the message you have just sent (step 11) and resend it to the same recipients:

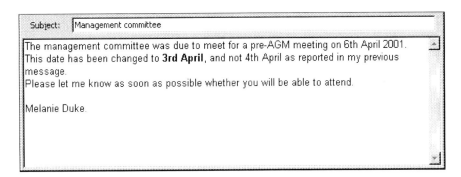

Subject: Management committee

The management committee was due to meet for a pre-AGM meeting on 6th April 2001. This date has been changed to **3rd April**, and not 4th April as reported in my previous message.
Please let me know as soon as possible whether you will be able to attend.

Melanie Duke.

▣13. Recall the message you have just sent (step 12) and ask to receive a message telling you whether you have been successful or not for each recipient.

14. Create the message shown below and define two voting buttons: **For** and **Against**. Address the message to the recipients of your choice (three in the **To** box) but do not send it.

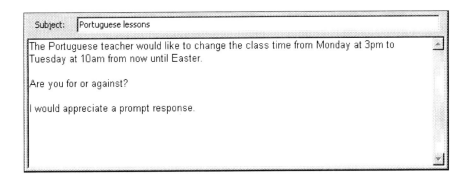

Subject: Portuguese lessons

The Portuguese teacher would like to change the class time from Monday at 3pm to Tuesday at 10am from now until Easter.

Are you for or against?

I would appreciate a prompt response.

You can always address the message to yourself if you cannot remember any e-mail addresses.

15. Define the tracking options for the active message (created in step 14) so that you are alerted when the message is read by the recipients then send the message.

16. Carry out the necessary actions so that users who try to contact you will receive a message telling them you are absent. The text to the autoreply should be: **I will be away until 10am tomorrow**.

    Close Outlook then re-open it and deactivate the out of office autoreply.

If you want to put what you have learned into practice in a real document, you can work on the summary exercise 2 for the E-MAIL section that you can find at the end of this book.

It is often possible to perform a task in several different ways, but here only the quickest solution is presented. Go back to the lesson to see the other techniques that can be used.

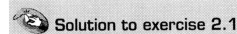

Solution to exercise 2.1

1. Display the contents of the **Sent Items** folder by opening the **My Shortcuts** group on the **Outlook** bar (click the appropriate button) then click the **Sent Items** folder.

   Show the contents of the **Deleted Items** folder by clicking the **Outlook Shortcuts** button on the **Outlook** bar, scrolling down the contents of the group using the ▼ button if necessary, and then clicking the **Deleted Items** folder.

   Select the **Inbox** folder by clicking the ▲ button to scroll up the **Outlook** bar if you need to and clicking the **Inbox** folder.

2. To create the first message and send it straight away, make sure you are in a message folder (such as the Inbox) and click ⊞ **New** ▾. Click in the **To** box, type the first recipient's address followed by a semi-colon then type the second address. Click in the **Cc** box and type the address for the person who is to receive a copy. In the **Subject** box, type **Easter holiday**. Click in the large text box and refer to the first illustration for the message text. When you have finished, click ✉ **Send**.

   For the second message, which you are going to save then correct and send later, be sure to be in a message folder (such as the Inbox) and click ⊞ **New** ▾. Click in the **To** box, type the first and second addresses, separating them with a semi-colon. Click the **Subject** box and type **Skiing trip** then click in the large text box and refer to the second illustration for the message text. When you have finished, click [icon] to save the message in the **Drafts** folder then press [Alt][F4] to close the message.

3. To check the spelling in the **Skiing trip** message in the **Drafts** folder, open the **My Shortcuts** group on the **Outlook** bar, click the **Drafts** folder and double-click the **Skiing trip** message. Place the insertion point at the beginning of the message text and use **Tools - Spelling**. For "shortlizt", click the **Change** button to replace it with "shortlist", for "Italie", choose "Italy" in the **Suggestions** box then click **Change**, and for "knoh", choose "know" in the **Suggestions** and click **Change**. Click **OK** once the spelling check in finished.

To apply bold type and font size 12 to the words French Alps, Italy (Dolomites) and Canada (Rockies), select this text, click the [B] tool to apply **Bold** type then open the [10] list and click **12** to apply a size 12 font.

To insert a bullet point in front of the three paragraphs containing French Alps, Italy (Dolomites) and Canada (Rockies) then increase the left indent, start by selecting the three paragraphs. Click the [icon] tool to insert the bullet points then the [icon] tool to increase the left indent.

To finish, click the [Send] button to send the message.

4. To create the message shown in step 4 of the exercise using stationery, use **Actions - New Mail Message Using - More Stationery**. Select a **Stationery** and click **OK**.

Click in the **To** box and type the recipients' addresses then click in the **Subject** box and type **Celebration**.

Click in the big text box and refer to the step 4 illustration for the main message text then click the [Send] button to send the message when you have finished.

⊞ 5. To create the message template shown in step 5, first click [⊞ New ▼]. To define the recipient of messages based on this template, enter a name in the **To** box.

Click in the **Subject** field and type **Activity sheet**. Now click in the large text box and refer to the step 5 illustration for the message contents.

Use **File - Save As**, delete the contents of the **File name** text box and type **Activity sheet**. Open the **Save as type** list and choose **Outlook Template (*.oft)**. Save the message.

Close the message window by clicking [✕] and click **No** when you are asked if you want to save the changes.

To create a message using the **Activity sheet** template, use **File - New - Choose Form**. Open the **Look in** list and click **User Templates in File System**. Select the **Activity sheet** template then click **Open**.

Complete the message as shown in step 5 then click [⊟ Send].

⊞ 6. To create the **Short** and **Long** signatures containing the information specified in step 6, be in the main Outlook window and use **Tools - Options**. Click the **Mail Format** tab then the **Signature Picker** button.

Create the **Short** signature by clicking the **New** button. Type **Short** in the **Enter a name for your new signature** box and click **Next**. Click in the first text box and type your **Name** and **Surname**. To apply bold type to your name and surname, select them and click the **Font** button. Choose the **Bold** option from the **Style** list then click **OK**. Confirm the signature by clicking **Finish**.

To create the **Long** signature, click the **New** button in the **Signature Picker**. Type **Long** in the **Enter a name for your new signature** box and click **Next**. Click in the first text box and type your **Name** and **Surname**, press ↵ and type your **Tel.:** followed by your phone number, press ↵ again, type **e-mail** then your e-mail address. To apply bold type to your name and surname, select them and click the **Font** button. Choose the **Bold** option from the **Style** list then click **OK**. Confirm the signature by clicking **Finish** then click **OK** in the **Signature Picker** dialog box.

So that neither of these signatures is the default signature, open the **Use this signature by default** list and choose **<None>**.

Finish by clicking **OK** to confirm the settings in the **Options** dialog box.

To create a new message using the **Activity sheet** template then insert the Short signature after the text "Feel free to…", use **File - New - Choose Form**. Open the **Look In** list and choose **User Templates in File System**. Click the **Activity sheet** template and click **Open**. Place the insertion point after the text "Feel free to…" and use **Insert - Signature**. Click **Short**.

7. To insert 2-1 Activity week 1.xls from the MOUS Outlook 2000 folder into the current message (the one you created in the previous step) after the "Feel free to…" text, place the insertion point after the text **Feel free to…** and click the ‖ tool.

Open the **Look In** list and choose the drive that contains the CD-ROM files supplied with this book then double-click the **MOUS Outlook 2000** folder. Select **2-1 Activity week 1.xls** and click **Insert**.

Send the message by clicking ⊡ Send .

8. To create the message shown in step 8 of the exercise, make sure you are in a message folder (such as the Inbox) and click ▣ New ▾ .

Click in the **To** box and type the recipient's address then click in the **Subject** box and type **Activity sheet week 1 message**.

Click in the big text box and refer to the step 8 illustration for the message text.

To insert the Outlook item that corresponds to the last message you sent as an attachment, place the insertion point after the message text and use **Insert - Item**. Choose the **Sent Items** folder in the **Look in** list then the first message in the **Items** list (the message subject is **Activity sheet** and the message has an attachment). Make sure **Attachment** is the active option and click **OK**.

Send the message by clicking ⊡ Send .

9. To create the message shown in step 9 of the exercise using Microsoft Word, first make sure you are in a message folder (such as the Inbox) then use **Actions - New Mail Message Using - Microsoft Office** and take the **Microsoft Word Document** option.

Click in the **To** box and type the recipient's address then click in the **Subject** and type **Spanish exam times**.

Click in the big text box and type the first paragraph (Below is...oral exam), press ⏎, type the second paragraph (Please inform...any problems) and press ⏎ twice.

Insert the table using **Table - Insert - Table**, enter **2** in the **Number of columns** text box and **6** in the **Number of rows** box then click **OK**. Complete the table by clicking in each cell and entering the information shown in the step 9 illustration.

Finish typing the message text by placing the insertion point under the table and typing **Karen Jones**.

Send the message by clicking the [≡ Send a Copy] button.

To close Microsoft Word without saving the message contents as a Word file, use **File - Exit** and click **No** when you are asked if you want to save the changes.

10. To create the message shown in step 10 of the exercise and select the recipients from an address book, make sure you are in a message folder (such as the Inbox) and click [New ▾] then [To...].

If necessary, open the **Show Names from the** list and click the address book you want to use.

For each main recipient (in the **To** box), choose the name from the list under **Type Name or Select from List** and click the [To ->] button. To add the name of the person who is to receive a copy (the **Cc** box), select their name from those under **Type Name or Select from List** and click [Cc ->]. Click **OK** to confirm the options in the **Select Names** dialog box.

Click in the **Subject** field and type **Management committee** then click in the large text box and refer to the step 10 illustration for the main message text.

11. To add a follow up flag to the active message telling the recipients you expect a reply in no more than 7 days, use **Actions - Flag for Follow Up**. Open the **Flag for** list and choose **Reply**. Now open the **Due by** list and select the date seven days from today's date. Click **OK**.

Click ⊟Send to send the message.

12. To change the text of the message you sent in step 11 so that it corresponds to the message shown in step 12 of the exercise, first open the **My Shortcuts** group by clicking the corresponding button in the **Outlook** bar. Click the **Sent Items** folder and click the **Management committee** message at the top of the list.

Use **Actions - Resend This Message**, select the text **4th April**, press Del and type **3rd April, and not 4th April as reported in my previous message**. Select **3rd April** and click the **B** to apply bold formatting.

Click ⊟Send to resend the message and close the old message window by clicking ✕.

13. To recall the message you sent in step 12 and ask to be informed whether you were successful for each recipient, make sure the **Sent Items** folder in the **My Shortcuts** group in selected. Double-click the first item in the **Sent Items** folder, the message with **Management committee** as the subject, and use **Actions - Recall This Message**.

Activate the **Delete unread copies of this message** option, make sure that **Tell me if recall succeeds or fails for each recipient** is active and click **OK**.

Close the message window by clicking ✕.

14. To create the message shown in step 14 of the exercise, make sure you are in a message folder (such as the Inbox) and click ![New ▾]. Click in the **To** box and enter the addresses of three recipients then click in the **Subject** and type **Portuguese lessons**. Click in the large text box and refer to the step 14 illustration for the main message text.

Use **View - Options** to define the For and Against voting buttons. Click in the **Use voting buttons** text box and type **For;Against**. Click **Close** to confirm the **Message Options** dialog box.

15. To define tracking options for the active message so that you will be notified when the recipients have read the message, use **View - Options**, activate **Request a read receipt for this message** and click **Close**.

Click ![Send] to send the message.

16. To inform those users who try to contact you that you are absent, by means of an automatic reply, first make sure you are in a message folder (such as the Inbox) then use **Tools - Out of Office Assistant**.

Activate the **I am currently Out of Office** option, click the **AutoReply only once to each sender with the following text** box and type **I will be away until 10am tomorrow**. Finish by clicking **OK**.

Close Outlook by clicking the ![X] button in the top right hand corner of the Outlook screen.

Open Outlook again by clicking **Start** on the task bar, selecting the **Programs** menu and clicking **Microsoft Outlook**.

Now click **Yes** when you are asked whether you want to deactivate the out of office assistant.

.

E-MAIL
Lesson 2.2: Receiving messages

1 ▪ Reading a message you have received

⁕ Activate the **Outlook Shortcuts** group and select the **Inbox** folder.

Unread messages are shown in bold and preceded by this symbol: ✉ .

⁕ If necessary, open the preview pane (**View - Preview Pane**) and click the message you want to read, or open the message by double-clicking it.

*It is possible that you will see a message telling you that new e-mail has just arrived (if you have activated the **Display a notification message when new mail arrives** option in the **E-mail Options** dialog box: **Tools - Options - Preferences** tab - **E-mail Options** button. If this is the case, you have two possibilities:*

*- click **Yes** to open the message and read it.*

*- click **No** if you do not want to read the message straight away, in which case it will appear in bold in the Inbox.*

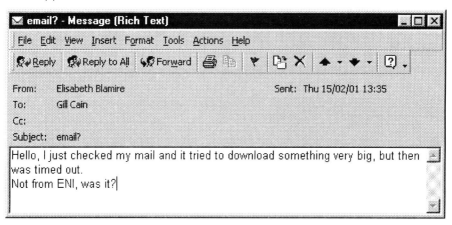

When you double-click a message it appears in a new window that contains, amongst other things, the sender's name and those of the recipients.

⁕ Use the ⬇ and ⬆ buttons to read the next or previous messages.

* When you have finished reading a message, click the ☒ button on the message window to close it.

*As soon as you have looked at a message it is considered as read and is preceded by this symbol: ✉. The message header is no longer shown in bold. If you want a message you have already opened to be shown as unread, right-click the message and choose **Mark as Unread**. The **Mark as Read** option will show an unopened message as read.*

*To make it easier to see your unread messages you can use the **View - Current View - Unread Messages** command. Once a message has been opened then closed it disappears from the list, of course.*

▪ Replying to a message

* Activate the **Outlook Shortcuts** group and click the **Inbox** folder.

* Open the message to which you want to reply by double-clicking it, or simply select it without opening it.

* To reply to the sender use **Actions - Reply** or [Reply] or [Ctrl] **R**.

* To reply to the sender and all the recipients, use **Actions - Reply to All** or [Reply to All] or [Ctrl] [Shift] **R**.

*A reply window (**RE**) opens: Outlook takes the sender of the original message as the recipient of the reply and the characters **RE** precede the subject. The text from the original message is present in the message window, preceded by the words **Original Message**.*

* Type your reply in the text box (above the original message text).

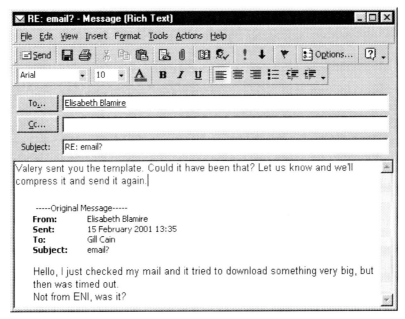

Notice that the reply text is blue. There is nothing to stop you from changing the original text. Any changes you make in the original text are also shown in blue and preceded by default by your user name.

※ Click **Send** to send your reply.

In the original message, Outlook reminds you of the date and time you replied to the message:

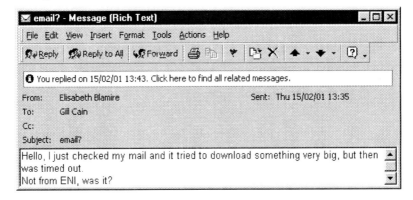

▫ Click to close the original message window.

*In your **Inbox**, the message is preceded by this symbol* 🖂 *and in your **Sent Items** folder the letters **RE** precede the message.*

📄 *To change the text that appears before changes you make to the original message text, activate the **Mark my comments with** option in the **E-mail Options** dialog box (**Tools - Options - Preferences** tab - **E-mail Options** button), type the new text in the box to the right of the **Mark my comments with** option then click **OK**.*

3 ▪ Replying to a message by voting

▫ Open the message asking you to vote by double-clicking it.

*The recipients know that they are being asked to vote because Outlook shows the words **Please respond using the buttons above.***

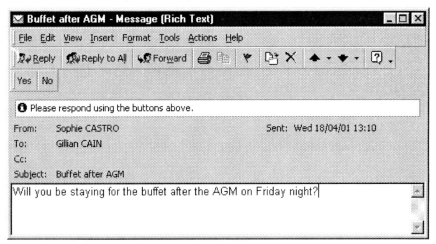

*This example shows a **Yes; No** vote, with corresponding buttons.*

▫ Click the button appropriate to your choice.

Outlook shows your choice and asks if you want to add comments to your vote.

* **Send the response now** or **Edit the response before sending** by activating the corresponding option then click **OK**.

* If you have chosen to edit the response before you send it, type your comments in the big text box that appears then click 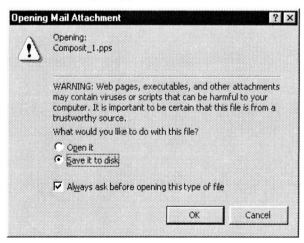 ▤ Send .

* Click the ▣ button to close the original message.

  *In the sender's **Sent Items** folder and the recipient's **Inbox** the vote response precedes the message subject.*

▥4 ▪ Managing message attachments

Opening an attached file

* Activate the **Outlook Shortcuts** group and choose the **Inbox**.

* Open the message that contains the attachment you want to open.

* Double-click the file icon.

  When you open the file, its source application is started, if possible. The dialog box below might appear:

The **Save it to disk** option allows you to save the file. The file does not open automatically once it has been saved. To open it, double-click the file icon again so that the **Opening Mail Attach-ment** reappears then choose **Open it**.

* Activate the **Open it** option.

※ If you do not want to see this message again, deactivate the **Always ask before opening this type of file** option.

※ Click **OK**.

※ After you have finished reading the file and made any changes, close the program by clicking ☒.

※ If you have made changes to the file a message will appear asking if you want to save them: click **Yes** to save the changes and close the application or **No** if you want to close the application without saving the changes.

If you have chosen to save the changes, they are saved in the file that corresponds to the attachment and is stored in the temporary folder C:\WINDOWS\TEMP. The changes will be visible the next time you open the attached document.

※ Finish by clicking ☒ to close the message window.

Saving attachments

※ Open the message containing the attachment to save.

※ **File - Save Attachments**

If the message contains more than one attachment, a dialog box appears, displaying a list of all the attachments. By default, they are all selected.

※ If you want to save all the attachments, click **OK**. Otherwise, ⌷Ctrl-click to select the ones to save and then click **OK**.

※ Select the drive and the folder where you want to save the attachments, then click the **Save** button.

※ Close the message window by clicking its ☒ button.

📄 *If you only need to save one of the attachments, you could also right-click its icon and take the **Save As** option.*

Managing attachments

※ You can preview the contents of an attachment without running its source program by right-clicking the attachment icon and choosing the **Quick View** option.

*The file contents appear in a dedicated window called **Quick View**.*

※ To delete an attachment, click the document icon to select it and press the `Del` key.

※ Move an attachment by clicking the file icon then dragging it to its new position.

※ You can change an attachment's label by right-clicking the file icon and choosing the **Properties** option.
Type the new **Label** for the attachment in the corresponding text box and click **OK**.

※ Print an attachment by right-clicking the file icon and choosing the **Print** option.

5 ▪ Forwarding a message you have received

You can forward a message to another person who was not amongst the original recipients.

※ Open the message you want to forward by double-clicking it or just select it without opening it.

※ **Actions - Forward** or `Forward` or `Ctrl` **F**

*The forward window (**FW**) appears. The message's subject appears preceded by the letters **FW** and the **Original Message** is shown in the message text box.*

※ Type the addresses of the new recipients in the **To** and **Cc** fields.

※ If necessary, type your own comments in the text box.

As with a message reply, your comments are shown in blue and you can make changes to the original text.

※ Click the `Send` button to send the message.

The date and time you forwarded the message are shown in the original message window.

» Click the ☒ button to close the original message window.

 *In the sender's **Inbox** forwarded messages are preceded with this symbol and in the **Sent Items** folder, the subject is preceded by the letters **FW**. In the recipient's **Inbox** the subject of a forwarded message is preceded by the letters **FW**.*

Below you can see **Practice exercise 2.2**. This exercise is made up of 5 steps. If you do not know how to complete one of the steps, go back to the lesson to refer to the corresponding title. When you have finished, check your work by reading the **Solution** on the next page.

Steps that are likely to be tested on the exam are marked with a 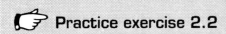 symbol. It is however recommended that you follow the whole exercice in order to gain a complete understanding of the lesson.

☞ Practice exercise 2.2

To complete exercise 2.2, create the three messages shown below on another computer and send them to yourself. If another computer is not available, create the messages on your own computer and send them.

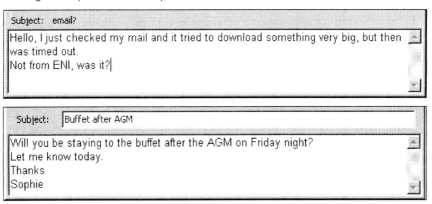

Subject: email?

Hello, I just checked my mail and it tried to download something very big, but then was timed out.
Not from ENI, was it?|

Subject: Buffet after AGM

Will you be staying to the buffet after the AGM on Friday night?
Let me know today.
Thanks
Sophie

*When you create the message, add **Yes** and **No** voting buttons.*

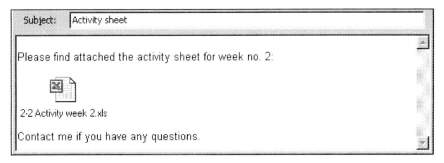

The **2-2 Activity week 2.xls** *file shown as an attachment in this message is from* the **MOUS Outlook 2000** *folder.*

Now return to your own computer.

1. Open the message with **email?** as the subject to read it.

   Once you have read the message, do not close it.

2. Reply to the sender of the open message as shown below:

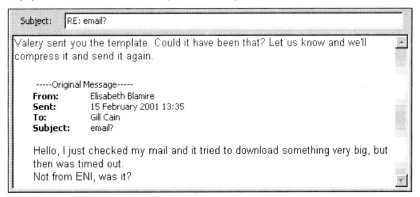

   Send the reply then close the original message window.

3. Open the message with **Buffet after AGM** as the subject and reply to the sender by voting **Yes**. Do not edit the reply before you send it.

   Close the original message when you have finished.

4. Open the message with **Activity sheet** as the subject and do the following:

- Display a quick preview of the attached document then close the preview window.

- Change the document's label to **Week 02/2001**.

- Open the attached document then, after consulting the file contents, close the application window.

- Print the attached document.

- Close the message window, remembering to save the changes.

5. Open the message with **Buffet after AGM** as the subject and forward it to the recipient of your choice (one address in the **To** field) without inserting any comments. If you cannot remember any e-mail addresses, forward the message to yourself.

Finish by closing the original message window.

If you want to put what you have learned into practice in a real document, you can work on the summary exercise 2 for the E-MAIL section that you can find at the end of this book.

It is often possible to perform a task in several different ways, but here only the quickest solution is presented. Go back to the lesson to see the other techniques that can be used.

 Solution to exercise 2.2

1. To open the message with "email?" as the subject so that you can read it, open the **Outlook Shortcuts** group by clicking the corresponding button on the **Outlook** bar then click the **Inbox** folder. Double-click the message whose subject is **email?** and read the message.

2. To reply to the sender of the open message, click the Reply button then type your reply as shown in the step **2** illustration. Click the Send button to send the message and close the original message window by clicking ✗.

3. Open the message you have received with the subject "Buffet after AGM" by clicking the button for the **Outlook Shortcuts** group in the **Outlook** bar then click the **Inbox** folder and double-click the **Buffet after AGM** message.
To reply to the message with a "Yes" vote, click the **Yes** button in the top of the screen, leave the **Send the response now** option active and click **OK**. Click ✗ to close the original message window.

4. In order to open the "Activity sheet" message, go to the **Outlook Shortcuts** group by clicking the corresponding button in the **Outlook** bar then click the **Inbox** folder. Double-click the message whose subject is **Activity sheet**.

   To see a quick preview of the attached file, right-click the document's icon and choose the **Quick View** option. Now close the preview window using **File - Close**.

Change the document's label to "Week 02/2001" by right-clicking the file icon and clicking the **Properties** option. Type **Week 02/2001** in the **Label** text box and click **OK**.

To open the document, double-click the icon. If necessary, choose the **Open it** option in the **Opening Mail Attachment** dialog box and click **OK**. After you have consulted the file's contents, close the application window by clicking the ☒ visible in the top right hand corner of the window.

Print the attached document by right-clicking the file icon and choosing **Print**.

To close the message and save the changes you have made, click the ☒ button then answer **Yes** to the message asking if you want to save the changes.

▦ 5. To open the message you have received whose subject is "Buffet after AGM" and forward it, make sure the **Inbox** folder in the **Outlook Shortcuts** group is selected and double-click the **Buffet after AGM** message then click Forward .

Click in the **To** box and type the recipient's address then click the button to send the message.

Close the original message window by clicking ☒.

E-MAIL
Lesson 2.3: Managing messages

▣1 ▪ Activating a standard view for message folders

Views allow you to present messages contained in message folders (such as the Inbox or Sent Items folders) in different ways.

▪ Select the message folder whose view you want to change.

▪ Use **View - Current View** or open the list associated with the **Current View** tool [Messages ▾].

▪ Click the option that corresponds to one of these views:

Messages	to see the messages as a list.
Messages with AutoPreview	to see the messages in a list showing the first three lines of the text of unread messages.
By Follow Up Flag	to see the messages in a list grouped by the follow up flag given to messages and with the due date of the follow up action for the messages.
Last Seven Days	to show a list of the messages received over the last seven days.
Flagged for Next Seven Days	to show flagged messages whose due dates fall in the next seven days.
By Conversation Topic	to see the messages in a list grouped by subject.
By Sender	to show messages in a list grouped by sender.
Unread messages	to see the messages in a list that contains only unread messages.
Sent To	to see a list of the messages showing the names of the recipients and not the senders.
Message Timeline	to see a list of messages shown as icons and placed according to the date they were sent.

2 ▪ Sorting messages

 ▪ Click the header of the column by which you want to sort.

The column is sorted immediately. Outlook inserts an arrowhead into the column header to show that a sort is active in the column.

▪ Click the header again to change the sort order.

📄 *This technique has the advantage of being quick but has two drawbacks: you can only define one sort criterion at a time and you can only sort according to the information that is visible.*

▪ Select the message folder that contains the messages you want to sort.

▪ **View - Current View - Customize Current View**

▪ Click the **Sort** button.

*As soon as the **Sort** dialog box opens you will notice that you can sort according to four different criteria at the same time.*

▪ For each sort criteria:

- select the name of the field that is to be the sort criterion. If the field you want is not available in the list, open the **Select available fields from** list and choose **All Mail fields**.

- indicate whether the sort is to be made in **Ascending** or **Descending** order by activating the appropriate option.

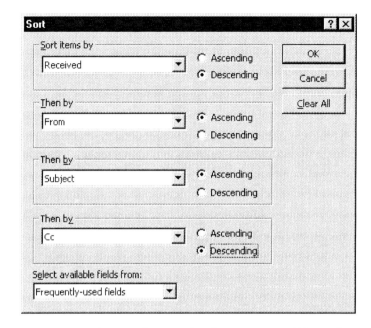

The messages are sorted according to the first criterion. When this value is the same for several items, they are sorted by the second criterion and so on.

⁂ Click **OK**.

If you select a field that is not shown in the view, Outlook asks you if you want to display it.

⁂ Click **Yes** to display the field or **No** if you do not want to.

 *To remove one or more sort criterion, use **View - Current View - Customize Current View** and click the **Sort** button. To remove a criterion, choose **(none)** in the appropriate list or remove all the criteria by clicking the **Clear All** button.*

3 ▪ Grouping messages

▪ Activate the folder that contains the messages you want to group.

▪ Open the **Group By** box by clicking this tool button: on the **Advanced** toolbar.

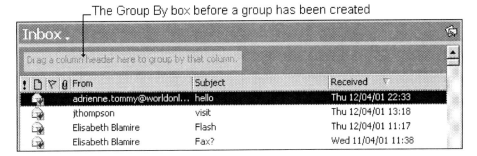

—The Group By box before a group has been created

▪ Drag the column header that corresponds to the field by which you want to group the messages to the Group By box.

▪ When the red arrows appear, release the mouse button.

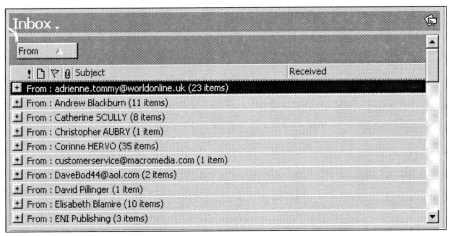

Straight away, the rows in the table are grouped and the name of the field is shown in the Group By box. You will notice that the column for that field is no longer visible.

To remove a group, drag the name of the field from the grouping box to its place among the column headers. If you do not remove the current group before creating a new one, you will in fact create a second level of grouping.

* Activate the folder that contains the messages you want to group.

* **View - Current View - Customize Current View**

* Click the **Group By** button.

* For each grouping criterion:

   - select the name of the field by which you want to group the messages. If the field you want is not available in the list, open the **Select available fields from** list and choose **All Mail fields**.

   - indicate whether you want the selected field to appear in the view by activating the **Show field in view** option.

   - decide whether the group should be in **Ascending** or **Descending** order by choosing the relevant option.

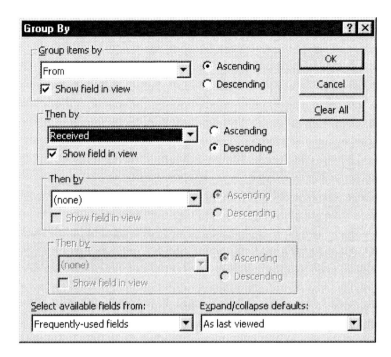

※ Open the **Expand/collapse defaults** list and click the option that corresponds to the way you want to see the groups: **As last viewed**, **All expanded** or **All collapsed**.

※ Click **OK** twice.

Grouping in this way systematically opens the group by box.

4 ▪ Expanding/collapsing groups of messages

When you group messages, each message group is preceded by a plus (+) sign.

※ To expand or collapse all the groups at once, use **View - Expand/Collapse Groups** and, depending on your choice, click **Collapse All** or **Expand All**.

- To expand one group, select the group and use **View - Expand/Collapse Groups - Expand This Group** or click the ⊞ button in front of the name of the group in question.

  All the messages in the group appear.

- Collapse a group by selecting it and using **View - Expand/Collapse Groups - Collapse This Group** or click the ⊟ button in front of the name of the group in question.

▣5 ▪ Printing message contents

- Activate the folder that contains the message(s) you want to print.

- Print a single message by selecting it or opening it. For several messages, select them using the `Shift` key for adjacent messages or the `Ctrl` key for non-adjacent messages.

- **File - Print** or `Ctrl` **P**

- In the **Print style** frame, choose **Memo Style**.

  *The **Table Style** prints a list of the messages but not their contents.*

- If you have selected several items, indicate whether you want to **Start each item on a new page** by activating the corresponding option in the **Print options** frame.

- If the messages contain attachments and you want to print them too, activate the **Print attached files with item(s)** option in the **Print options** frame.

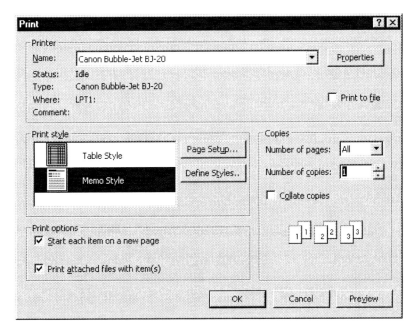

* To print odd and/or even pages, select the appropriate option in the **Number of pages** in the **Copies** frame.

* Type the number of copies you want to print in the **Number of copies** box in the **Copies** frame.

* Activate the **Collate copies** option to print the messages copy by copy and not page by page.

* Click **OK** to start printing.

The **Page Setup** button in the **Print** dialog box enables you to define the page setup for the selected print style and, in particular, to define headers and/or footers.

The tool prints an item immediately using the default settings in the **Print** dialog box.

You can see a print preview by clicking the ⬚ *tool button or by clicking the* **Preview** *button in the* **Print** *dialog box.*

.

⬚6 ▪ Filtering messages

Filtering messages means that you can display only those messages that fulfil your criteria.

▪ Select the folder that contains the messages you want to filter.

▪ **View - Current View - Customize Current View**

▪ Click the **Filter** button then, if necessary, the **Messages** tab.

▪ In the **Search for the word(s)** box, type the text you want to find.

If you want to use text you have already searched for, open the **Search for the word(s)** *list and choose the text.*

▪ Open the **In** list and click the option that corresponds to the field or fields in which you want to carry out the search.

▪ To use a filter to display messages received from one or more senders, type the corresponding address(es) in the **From** button text box or click the **From** to choose addresses from an address book.

▪ To use a filter to display messages sent to one or more recipients, type the addresses in the **Sent To** button text box or click the **Sent To** to select the corresponding addresses from an address book.

▪ To use a filter to display messages you have received, activate the **Where I am** option and click one of the options in the associated list:

The only person on the To line	to display the messages for which you are the sole recipient.
on the To line with other people	to display messages sent to you and other people.

on the CC line with other people to display messages sent with your address in the Cc box, along with other peoples.

* If you want to filter messages according to time criteria, use the two lists associated with the **Time** option.

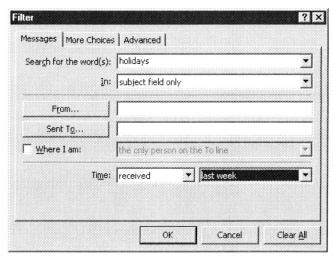

This filter will display only messages received last week that contain the word holidays.

* If you want to choose more filter criteria such as the file size or whether or not the messages have an attachment or you want to respect the case, click the **More Choices** tab and choose the criteria you want.

* To filter according to extra or custom fields, click the **Advanced** tab and choose the options you want.

* Click **OK** twice.

  *When a filter is active, Outlook signals this by showing the words **Filter Applied** on the left of the status bar. The total number of items in the folder is also shown.*

* You can remove all filters by using **View - Current View - Customize Current View**, click the **Filter** button then **Clear All** and then click **OK** twice.

7 ▪ Finding a message

Making a quick search

▪ Select the folder you want to search.

▪ **Tools - Find** or 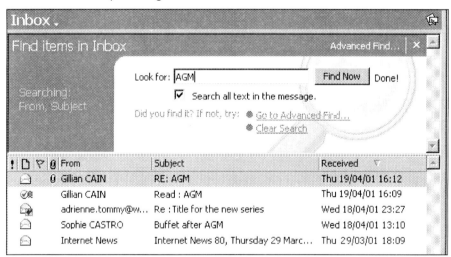 **Find**

*The **Find** window appears.*

▪ Type the text you want to **Look for** in the corresponding text box.

▪ Activate the **Search all text in the message** option if you want Outlook to search the whole message and not just the subject.

▪ Start the search by clicking **Find Now**.

Inbox ▾		
Find items in Inbox	Advanced Find...	✕

Look for: AGM   Find Now   Done!

☑ Search all text in the message.

Searching: From, Subject

Did you find it? If not, try: ● Go to Advanced Find...
                              ● Clear Search

!	🗋	▽	📎	From	Subject	Received ▽
	✉		📎	Gillian CAIN	RE: AGM	Thu 19/04/01 16:12
	✅			Gillian CAIN	Read : AGM	Thu 19/04/01 16:09
	✉			adrienne.tommy@w...	Re : Title for the new series	Wed 18/04/01 23:27
	✉			Sophie CASTRO	Buffet after AGM	Wed 18/04/01 13:10
	✉			Internet News	Internet News 80, Thursday 29 Marc...	Thu 29/03/01 18:09

In the lower part of the window, Outlook shows all the messages that contain the word "AGM" in the message subject or text.

▪ If you want to display all the messages in the folder again, click **Clear Search**. Click **Go to Advanced Find** to make a more defailed search.

* Close the **Find** window by using **Tools - Find** or click the ⌖ Find button or click the ⊠ button in the top right hand corner of the **Find** window.

*When you close the **Find** window, all the messages in the folder are displayed again.*

Making an advanced search

* Select the folder you want to search.

* **Tools - Advanced Find** or Ctrl Shift **F**

*You can also click the **Advanced Find** link in the **Find** window.*

* If necessary, click the **Messages** tab.

* In the **Look for** list in the top of the dialog box, select the **Messages** option.

* Make sure the name of the folder you want to search is shown in the **In** text box. If this is not the case, or if you want to search several message folders, click the **Browse** button then tick the boxes for each folder you want to search and untick the rest. Click **OK**.

*If you tick the **Inbox** folder in the **Select Folder(s)** dialog box, all the folders in your mailbox will be searched.*

* In the **Search for the word(s)** text box on the **Messages** tab, type the words you want to find.

*To use text you have already searched for, open the **Search for the word(s)** list and click the appropriate text.*

* Open the **In** list and click the option that corresponds to the field or fields you want to search.

* To look for messages received from one or more senders, type the corresponding address(es) in the **From** text box or click the **From** button to choose addresses from an address book.

- To look for messages sent to one or more e-mail addresses (recipients), type the addresses in the **Sent To** text box or click the **Sent To** button to select the corresponding addresses from an address book.

- To look for messages you have received, activate the **Where I am** option and click one of the options in the associated list:

The only person on the To line	to look for messages for which you are the sole recipient.
on the To line with other people	to look for messages sent to you and other people.
on the CC line with other people	to look for messages sent with your address in the Cc box, along with other people's.

- If you want to find messages according to time criteria, use the two lists associated with the **Time** option.

- If you want to choose more search criteria such as the file size or whether or not the messages have an attachment, or if you want to respect the case, click the **More Choices** tab and choose the criteria you want.

- To find messages by criteria based on extra or custom fields, click the **Advanced** tab and choose the options you want.

- Click the **Find Now** button.

If the search is successful, the messages found are shown in the lower part of the window:

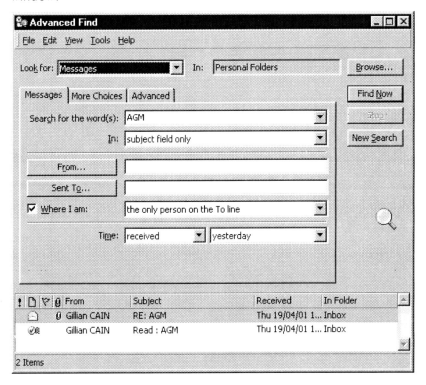

If this is not the case, a message appears: **There are no items to show in this view**.

» Open one of the messages found by double-clicking it.

» You can remove the search criteria and start a new search by clicking the **New Search** button. Click **OK** to the message telling you that your current search criteria will be deleted.

» Close a search using **File - Close** or press ⎡Alt⎤⎡F4⎤ or click the ⌧ button in the search window.

You can save your search criteria, so that you can use them again, using **File - Save Search**. *Give a name for the file (with an .oss extension). To re-use the search, go to the* **Advanced Search** *dialog box (***Tools - Advanced Search***) and open the oss file using* **File - Open Search**.

8 ▪ Customising the current view

Managing fields in a view

Amongst other things, a view is defined by the fields it contains. Each field contains specific information.

※ Select the folder whose fields you want to reorganize.

※ **View - Current View - Customize Current View**

※ Click the **Fields** button.

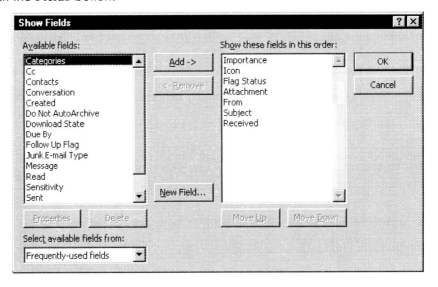

*In the window that opens, the **Available fields** list shows all the fields you can use and the **Show these fields in this order** box shows a list of the fields used in the view. The contents of the **Available fields** list depends on the option selected in the **Select available fields from** list.*

※ To add a new field, select the field that will precede it in the **Show these fields in this order** list.

Select the list of fields you want from the **Select available fields from** drop-down list.

Now choose the field you want in the **Available fields** and click the **Add** button.

You can also add a field by double-clicking its name.

※ Delete a field by selecting it in the **Show these fields in this order** list and clicking **Remove**.

※ Move a field by selecting it in the **Show these fields in this order** list and using the **Move Up** or **Move Down** buttons.

You can also move a field by dragging it up or down the list.

※ Create a field by clicking the **New Field** button.

Give the field a **Name** in the corresponding text box, select the **Type** then, if necessary, choose a **Format**, using the corresponding drop-down lists.

Click **OK**.

Changing fonts

※ Select the folder in which you want to change the font.

- **View - Current View - Customize Current View**

- Click the **Other Settings** button.

- Change the font, style, size and/or script of the column headers by clicking the **Font** button in the **Column headings** frame and selecting the options you want before clicking **OK**.

- To change the font, style, size and/or script of the rows (one row corresponds to one message), click the **Font** button in the **Rows** frame, select the options you want and click **OK**.

- To change the font, style, size and/or script of the auto preview, click the **Font** in the **AutoPreview** frame, select the options you want and click **OK**.

- Click **OK** twice.

Authorising direct editing

Activating this option allows you to change the contents of a cell simply by clicking in the cell.

- Select the folder in which you want to allow direct editing.

- **View - Current View - Customize Current View**

- Click the **Other Settings** button.

- Activate the **Allow in-cell editing** option in the **Rows** frame.

- Click **OK** twice.

Changing the column width

- Point to the vertical line at

- the left at the header of the column you want to change.

- Drag to change the column width.

- You can also adjust the column's width to fit its contents by double-clicking it.

  Be careful, some columns have fixed widths.

*If you would rather apply a precise width, right-click the column header and click the **Format columns** option. In the **Specific width** text box, give the width you want and click **OK**.*

Changing the order of the columns

» Activate the folder in which you want to change the column order.

» Click the header of the column you want to move and drag it left or right.

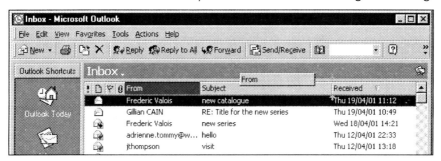

Outlook indicates the new position with two red arrows. If you are trying to move the header to an invalid position, Outlook places a big black cross over the column header. If you release the mouse button while the cross is visible, the field will disappear from the view.

» When the arrows are in the right place, release the mouse button.

Adding a column

» Select the folder in which you want to add a column.

» Click the tool button on the **Advanced** toolbar.

» Click the name of the field you want to add and drag it to its position on the column headings row.

*If the field you want is not visible in the list of fields, open the drop-down list in the top of the window and click the **All Mail fields** option.*

» When the field is in the desired position, release the mouse button.

» Close the **Field Select** window by clicking ☒.

Creating a field

» Select the folder in which you want to create a field.

» Click the ⊡ tool button on the **Advanced** toolbar and click the **New** button.

» Give the **Name**, **Type** and **Format** of the field in the appropriate text boxes and click **OK**.

» Close the **Field Selector** window by clicking ☒.

Deleting a column

» Select the folder in which you want to delete a column.

» Click the column header and drag it off the column header row until Outlook places a big black cross over it: _{From} ✕ .

» Release the mouse button.

Changing the alignment of column contents

» Select the folder in which you want to change the alignment of the column contents.

» **View - Current View - Format Columns**

» In the **Available Fields** list, select the field for the column you want to change.

» Activate the **Left**, **Center** or **Right** option in the **Alignment** frame and click **OK**.

📄 *You can also right-click the column header, click the **Alignment** option then the option you want.*

Changing the labels of the column headings

- Select the folder in which you want to change the column heading labels.
- **View - Current View - Format Columns**
- In the **Available Fields** list, select the field for the column whose label you want to change.

*The labels of some fields, such as **Importance** or **Attachment**, cannot be changed.*

- Type the column heading's new **Label** in the corresponding text box and click **OK**.

Changing the format of columns containing dates

You can change the way in which dates are shown in the column.

- **View - Current View - Format Columns**
- In the **Available Fields** list, select the field whose date format you want to change.
- Open the **Format** list and click the option that corresponds to the date format you want then click **OK**.

Changing the appearance of rows

- Select the folder in which you want to change the appearance of the rows.
- **View - Current View - Customize Current View**
- Click the **Other Settings** button.

*Here you want to use the **Grid lines** frame.*

- Open the **Grid line style** list and choose the type of line you want.
- In the **Grid line color** list, choose the colour you want for the grid lines.

This option is unavailable if you do not choose a line style.

※ You can apply a shadow to group headings by activating the **Shade group headings** option.

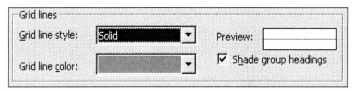

※ Click **OK**.

9 ▪ Manually archiving messages

You can avoid building up a lot of messages in your folders, especially your Inbox, by moving messages elsewhere for storage. You can do this manually or automatically (see next section).

※ **File - Archive**

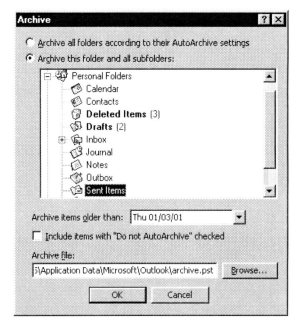

- Leave the **Archive this folder and all subfolders** option active then click the folder you want to archive.

- Open the **Archive items older than** list and select the cut off date for the archiving.

- Activate the **Include items with "Do not AutoArchive" checked** option if you want to archive items that are marked **Do not AutoArchive**.

- Leave the default **Archive file** name or type another name in the text box.

  *You can click **Browse** to select the archive file.*

- Click **OK**.

  *Archived items disappear from their original folder. You can see them by displaying the folder list, expanding the **Archive Folders** then clicking the folder in question.*

10 ▪ Managing AutoArchive

Unless the setting is changed, Outlook runs the AutoArchive process every 14 days at start-up. This process opens this window:

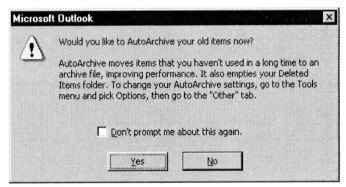

Each folder has its own autoarchive rules.

Defining the AutoArchive at start-up rules

* **Tools - Options**

* Click the **Other** tab then the **AutoArchive** button.

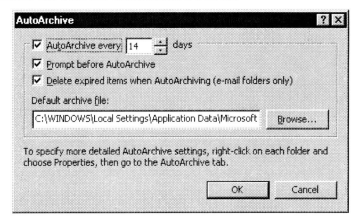

* In the **AutoArchive every** text box, type the number of days that should go by between each autoarchive.

  *If you deactivate this option or type **0** in the text box, the AutoArchive at start-up will be deactivated.*

* Indicate whether Outlook should **Prompt before AutoArchive** or not, by activating or deactivating the corresponding option.

* Activate the **Delete expired items when AutoArchiving (e-mail folders only)** if certain items whose expiry dates have passed should be deleted during archiving.

* Leave the default **Default archive file** name or type another name in the text box.

  *You can click **Browse** to select the archive file.*

* Click **OK**.

Defining AutoArchive rules for a folder

⁎ Select the folder whose AutoArchive rules you want to define.

⁎ **File - Folder - Properties for "name of folder"**

⁎ Click the **AutoArchive** tab.

⁎ If necessary, activate the **Clean out items older than** option.

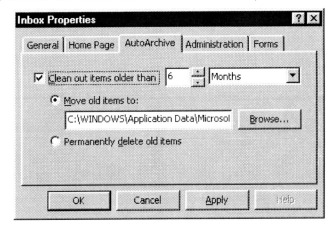

⁎ In the **Clean out items older than** text box and list, indicate how old an item should be before it can be archived automatically.

⁎ Leave the **Move old items to** option active and, if necessary, change the name of the archive file by typing a different name in the text box or clicking the **Browse** button to select a new file/location.

⁎ Click **OK**.

Defining a message's autoarchive settings

⁎ Open the message in question.

⁎ **File - Properties**

⁎ Click the **General** tab and activate **Do not AutoArchive this item**.

⁎ Click **OK**.

11 ▪ Importing archived items

▪ **File - Import and Export**

▪ Select the **Import from another program or file** in the **Choose an action to perform** list.

▪ Click **Next**.

▪ Select the **Personal Folder File (.pst)** option and click **Next**.

▪ In the **File to import** text box type the path for the archive file or click **Browse** and select it.

▪ Indicate how duplicate items should be treated by choosing from the choices in the **Options** frame: **Replace duplicates with items imported**, **Allow duplicates to be created** or **Do not import duplicates**.

▪ Click **Next** and select the folder you want to import.

▪ If necessary, click the **Filter** button to define conditions for selecting the items to be imported.

▪ If you want the items to be imported into the active folder, activate the **Import items into the current folder** option, or, to import the items into their original folders, activate **Import items into the same folder**.

▪ Click **Finish**.

12 ▪ Creating a folder

In Outlook, the are different types of folder:

- ***Outlook folders*** *or* ***private folders****: these folders contain Outlook items. You own these folders and can share them with other users.*

- ***public folders*** *can be used to share information within your company and also over the Internet through newsgroups. They are created and managed by the network administrator who can define permissions for users. These folders are only available if you are working with Microsoft Exchange Server.*

You can see these folders if you display the folder list (see Lesson 1.1: Discovering the environment).

※ **File - Folder - New Folder** or Ctrl Shift **E**

※ Give the new folder's **Name** in the corresponding text box.

※ Make sure the **Mail Items** option is selected in the **Folder contains** list; this option indicates that you want to store messages in the folder you are creating.

※ In the **Select where to place the folder** list, choose the folder in which the new folder should be created.

This place does not have any effect on the position of the folder shortcut.

※ Click **OK**.

※ Answer **Yes** or **No** when Outlook asks **Would you like a shortcut to this folder added to your Outlook bar?**. If you accept, the shortcut is placed in the **My Shortcuts** group.

13 ▪ Deleting/renaming a folder

※ Select the folder concerned. If it does not have a shortcut, open the folder list (**View - Folder List** or ⊞) and select it.

※ To delete a folder use **File - Folder - Delete "name of folder"** or press Del. Click **Yes** to confirm.

*If a shortcut had been created for the folder on the **Outlook** bar, you will notice that it is still visible in the **My Shortcuts** group of the Outlook bar. You can delete this shortcut if you want. Right-click the shortcut and choose the **Remove from Outlook Bar** option then confirm the deletion by clicking **Yes**.*

※ To rename a folder, use **File - Folder - Rename "name of folder"**, change the name and press ↵ to confirm.

This action only changes the folder's name; any shortcut to the folder will remain unchanged.

14 ▪ Copying/moving messages in a folder

✳ Activate the folder that contains the messages you want to move/copy and select the messages, using [Shift] to select adjacent messages or [Ctrl] for non-adjacent ones.

✳ **Edit - Copy to Folder** or **Edit - Move to Folder** or [Ctrl] [Shift] **V**

✳ Select the destination folder or create one by clicking the **New** button.

✳ Click **OK**.

> 🔍 *You can also drag the selected messages to the destination folder on the Outlook bar or in the folder list. To copy the messages, hold the* [Ctrl] *key down as you drag. The* **Tools - Organize** *command (or* [🔲 Organize] *button) is another way to move messages. You can use these techniques to recover an item you have deleted by accident: move the item from* **Deleted Items** *to the appropriate folder.*

15 ▪ Turning a message into a different type of Outlook item

Turning a message into an appointment or event

✳ Select the message you want to convert to an appointment or event and drag it to the **Calendar** shortcut in the **Outlook Shortcuts** group on the **Outlook** bar.

As soon as you release the mouse, the **Appointment** *window opens and the message contents are shown in the big text box.*

✳ If necessary, indicate the different characteristics of the appointment. If it is an event, activate the **All day event** option.

✽ Click the [💾 Save and Close] button.

Turning a message into a task

✽ Select the message in question and drag it on to the **Tasks** shortcut in the **Outlook Shortcuts** group on the **Outlook** bar.

The task creation window opens straight away.

✽ Type in the information for this task then click [💾 Save and Close].

Turning a message into a note

✽ Open the message then select the text that is to be inserted into the note. For example, you might select the subject only, or perhaps the whole message.

If you want to use the whole message in the note, you do not need to open it. Simply click the message to select it.

✽ Drag your selection onto the **Notes** shortcut in the **Outlook Shortcuts** group on the **Outlook** bar.

Straight away, a new note window appears containing the text of the selection.

✽ If necessary, you can type some additional text to complete the note.

✽ Click the ✖ button to close the note.

Below you can see **Practice exercise 2.3**. This exercise is made up of 15 steps. If you do not know how to complete one of the steps, go back to the lesson to refer to the corresponding title. When you have finished, check your work by reading the **Solution** on the next page.

Steps that are likely to be tested on the exam are marked with a symbol. It is however recommended that you follow the whole exercice in order to gain a complete understanding of the lesson.

☞ Practice exercise 2.3

1. Change the view in the **Sent Items** folder so that you can only see messages sent over the last seven days.
   Change the view in the **Inbox** so that the messages are grouped according to the sender.
   Now display all the messages in both the **Inbox** and **Sent Items** folders.

2. Use the menu method to sort the messages in the **Inbox** folder in ascending order according to the sender (**From** field) then in ascending order according to the date they were received (**Received** field).
   Now use the mouse to sort the messages in the **Inbox** folder in descending order according to the date they were received (**Received** field).

3. Use the menu method to group the messages in the **Inbox** by ascending order of senders (**From** field) then by descending order of the date they were received (**Received** field). The fields used for grouping should be shown in the view.

4. Expand all the groups at once. Now collapse one group then all the groups at once. Finish by removing all the groups.

5. Print two copies of the contents of the **Buffet after AGM** and **Activity sheet** messages in the **Inbox** folder. You should print one message per page and the contents of the attachment to the **Activity sheet** message should also be printed.

6. Filter the messages in the **Inbox** so that only those messages addressed exclusively to you and received over the last seven days are shown. Now remove the filter.

7. In the **Inbox**, find the message whose subject contains the word **AGM**.

   Finish by closing the **Find** window.

8. Change the view in the **Inbox** by making the following changes:

   - Add the **Cc** field after the **Attachment** field.

   - Adjust the width of the **From** column to fit its contents.

   - Change the column order so that the **Cc** column is between the **From** and **Subject** columns.

   - Add the **Size** column to the right of the **Cc** column.

   - Centre the contents of the **Cc** and **Size** columns.

   - Change the label of the **Cc** field to **Copy**.

   - Delete the **Copy** and **Size** columns.

9. In the **Sent Items** folder, manually archive the messages that are older than one month. You should leave the default file name (C:\WINDOWS\ Application Data\Microsoft\Outlook\archive.pst).

10. Define the AutoArchive settings so that messages are archived at start-up every **12** days.

   Make the necessary changes to ensure that messages in the **Inbox** with

   Activity sheet as the subject cannot be archived.

11. Import the messages you manually archived in step 9 (remember that these messages were archived in the default archive folder: C:\WINDOWS\ Application Data\Microsoft\Outlook\archive.pst). The imported items should replace duplicates and the messages should be imported into their original folder (the **Sent Items** folder).

12. Create **Training** and **Misc** folders in the **Inbox**.

    Do not create shortcuts to either of these folders on the **Outlook** bar.

13. Rename the **Training** folder **Outlook Training** and delete the **Misc** folder.

14. Copy all messages in the Inbox with either **email?** or **Activity sheet** as the subject to the **Outlook Training** folder. Check the contents of the **Outlook Training** folder then close the folder list.

15. Take the message with **Buffet after AGM** as the subject in the **Inbox** and turn it into an appointment. The appointment should begin next Friday at **17:00** and finish at **20:00**.

If you want to put what you have learned into practice in a real document, you can work on the summary exercise 2 for the E-MAIL section that you can find at the end of this book.

It is often possible to perform a task in several different ways, but here only the quickest solution is presented. Go back to the lesson to see the other techniques that can be used.

Solution to exercise 2.3

1. To change the view in the Sent Items folder so that you can only see the messages sent over the last seven days, open the **My Shortcuts** group by clicking the appropriate button on the **Outlook** bar then click the **Sent Items** folder. Use **View - Current View** and click **Last Seven Days**.

   In order to change the view in the Inbox so that the messages are grouped according to the sender, open the **Outlook Shortcuts** group by clicking the appropriate button on the **Outlook** bar then click the **Inbox** folder. Use **View - Current View** and click **By Sender**.

   To show all the messages in the Inbox again, use **View - Current View** and click the **Messages** option.

   So that all the messages in the **Sent Items** are displayed again, you need to go to the **My Shortcuts** group by clicking the corresponding button on the **Outlook** bar

   then click the **Sent Items** folder. Use **View - Current View** and click **Messages**.

2. To sort the messages in the Inbox by ascending order according to the sender (**From** field) then descending order according to the date they were received (**Received** field), open the **Outlook Shortcuts** group by clicking the corresponding button on the **Outlook** bar then click the **Inbox** folder. Use **View - Current View - Customize Current View** and click the **Sort** button.

   Open the list in the **Sort items by** frame and click the **From** option. Open the list in the **Then by** frame and choose **Received** from the end of the list.

Now activate the **Ascending** option in the **Then by** frame. Click **OK** to finish.

To sort the messages in the Inbox in descending order according to when they were received (**Received** field) using the mouse method, click the **Received** column header once.

3. To group the messages in the Inbox in ascending order according to the sender (**from** field) then by ascending order according to the date of reception (**Received** field), make sure that the **Inbox** folder in the **Outlook Shortcuts** group is selected. Use **View - Current View - Customize Current View** and click the **Group By** button.

Open the drop-down list in the **Group items by** frame and click the **From** option. In the **Then by** frame open the list and scroll down to select the **Received** option. Make sure that the **Show field in view** option is active for both the grouping criteria then click **OK** twice.

4. Expand all the groups at once using **View - Expand/Collapse Groups** and choose **Expand All**.

Collapse one group by clicking the ⊟ button in front of a group of your choice.

To collapse all the groups at once, use **View - Expand/Collapse Groups** and click **Collapse All**.

To remove all the groups, use **View - Current View - Customize Current View** and click the **Group By** button. Click the **Clear All** button then finish by clicking **OK**.

5. To print two copies of the contents of the messages you have received (in the Inbox) called Buffet after AGM and Activity sheet, make sure you are in the **Inbox** in the **Outlook Shortcuts** group. Click on the row with the **Activity sheet** message, hold the Ctrl key down and click on the row with the **Buffet after AGM** message. Run **File - Print** and make sure that **Memo Style** is selected in the **Print style** frame.

Type **2** in the **Number of copies** text box in the **Copies** frame to print two copies.

To print one message per page, makes sure the **Start each item on a new page** option is active in the **Print options** frame.

To print the contents of the attachment in the **Activity sheet** message, activate **Print attached files with item(s)** in the **Print options** frame.

Click **OK** to start the printing.

6. To filter the messages contained in the Inbox so that only those sent exclusively to you in the last seven days are visible, make sure the **Inbox** folder is selected. Use **View - Current View - Customize Current View** and click **Filter**.

Open the first list associated with the **Time** option and choose **received**. Open the second **Time** list and choose **in the last 7 days**. Activate the **Where I am** option and make sure that **The only person on the To line** option is visible in the corresponding drop-down list then click **OK** twice.

Remove the filter by using **View - Current View - Customize Current View**, click the **Filter** button then click **Clear All** and click **OK** twice.

7. To search the Inbox for all messages whose subjects contain the word "AGM", make sure you are in the **Inbox** folder in the **Outlook Shortcuts** group and click the [Find] button. Type the word **AGM** in the **Look for** text box, deactivate the **Search all text in the message** option if need be and click the **Find Now** button.
Close the **Find** window by clicking the ⊠ button in the top right corner of the window.

8. To change the view in the Inbox, make sure the **Inbox** folder in the **Outlook Shortcuts** is selected.

To add the Cc field after the Attachment field, use **View - Current View - Customize Current View** and click **Fields**. Select the **Attachment** field in the **Show these fields in this order** list, select the **Cc** in the **Available fields** list and click **Add**. Now click **OK** twice.

Adjust the width of the **From** column to fit its contents by placing the mouse pointer over the vertical line at the right of the **From** label and double-clicking.

To change the order of the columns so that the Cc column comes between the From and Subject columns, click the header of the **Cc** column and drag it to the right until it is between the **From** and **Subject** fields. Release the mouse button when the red arrows appear.

To add a **Size** column to the right of the **Cc** column, click the ⊞ tool button and scroll down the fields list until you can see the **Size** field then drag it to the right of the **Cc** on the column heading row. When the two red arrows appear, release the mouse button. Now close the **Field Selector** window by clicking ☒.

To centre the contents of the Cc and Size columns, use **View - Current View - Format Columns**. Select the **Cc** field in the **Available Fields** list and activate the **Center** option in the **Alignment** frame. Select the **Size** in the **Available Fields** list and activate the **Center** option in the **Alignment** frame then click **OK**.

Change the label of the Cc field to Copy using **View - Current View - Format Columns**. Select the **Cc** field in the **Available Fields** list, select the contents of the **Label** text box and press the [Del] key. Now type **Copy** and click **OK**.

Delete the Copy column by clicking the heading of the **Copy** field and dragging off the column headers row. When Outlook places a big black cross over the heading of the Copy field, release the mouse.

To delete the Size column, click the header of the **Size** field and drag it off the column header row. Release the mouse button when Outlook places a big black cross over the heading of the Size field.

▦ 9. Manually archive all the messages in the Sent Items folder that were sent over a month ago using **File - Archive**. Leave the **Archive this folder and all subfolders** option active and click the **Sent Items** folder.

Open the **Archive items older than** list and select the date that is a month earlier than today's date. Leave the default **Archive File** (C:\WINDOWS\ Application data\Microsoft\Outlook\archive.pst) in the corresponding text box and click **OK**.

▦10. To set the autoarchiving of messages at start-up to every 12 days, use **Tools - Options**, click the **Others** tab then the **AutoArchive** button. Select the contents of the **AutoArchive every** text box, press ⌷Del⌷, type **12** then click **OK** twice.

To prevent the "Activity sheet" message in the Inbox from being autoarchived, first make sure the **Inbox** folder in the **Outlook Shortcuts** group is selected then double-click the message with **Activity sheet** as the subject. Now use **File - Properties**, click the **General** tab, activate the **Do not AutoArchive this item** tab then click **OK**. Close the message by clicking ☒ and click **Yes** to the message asking if you want to save the changes.

▦11. To import the messages you manually archived in step 9, use **File - Import and Export**, select **Import from another program or file** from the **Choose an action to perform** list and click **Next**.

Select the **Personal File Folder (.pst)** option and click **Next**.

Leave the default file name (C:\WINDOWS\Application Data\Microsoft\ Outlook\archive.pst) in the **File to import** text box, make sure the **Replace duplicates with items imported** option is active in the **Options** and click **Next**.

Select the **Sent Items** folder, make sure the **Import items into the same folder in** option is active and click **Finish**.

12. To create a Training folder in the Inbox, use **File - Folder - New Folder**. Click in the **Name** text box and type **Training**. Make sure the **Mail Items** option is selected in the **Folder contains** list. Select the **Inbox** folder in the **Select where to place the folder** list and click **OK**. Click **No** when you are asked if you want to place a shortcut to the folder on the Outlook bar.

Create a Misc folder in the Inbox using **File - Folder - New Folder**. Click in the **Name** text box and type **Misc**. Make sure the **Mail Items** option is selected in the **Folder contains** list. Select the **Inbox** folder in the **Select where to place this folder** list and click **OK**. Click **No** when you are asked if you want to place a shortcut to the folder on the Outlook bar.

13. Rename the Training folder as Outlook Training by selecting the **Training** folder in the folder list then use **File - Folder - Rename "Training"**. Click before the word **Training**, type **Outlook**, press Space then press ⏎.

To delete the Misc folder, select it in the folder list and use **File - Folder - Delete "Misc"**. Click **Yes** to confirm deletion of the folder.

14. To copy messages from the Inbox with "email?" or "Activity sheet" as the subject to the Outlook Training folder, select the **Inbox** folder in the folder list. Click the message whose subject is **email**, and hold down the Ctrl key as you click the message whose subject is **Activity sheet**.

Use **Edit - Copy to Folder**, click the + sign you can see at the left of the Inbox folder, select the **Outlook Training** folder and click **OK**.

Check the contents of the Outlook Training folder by clicking **Outlook Training** in the folder list.

Click the ☒ button in the top right corner of the folder list to close it.

15. To transform the Buffet message in the Inbox into an appointment, make sure the **Inbox** folder is active. Click the message whose subject is **Buffet after AGM** and drag it to the **Calendar** shortcut in the **Outlook Shortcuts** group.

Indicate the day of the appointment by opening the **Start time** list and clicking the date of next Friday.

Set the appointment's starting time to 5 pm by opening the second list associated with the **Start time** option and clicking **17:00**.

Set the end time of the appointment to 8 pm by opening the second **End time** list and choosing **20:00 (3 hours)**.

Finish creating the appointment by clicking 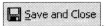.

.

THE CALENDAR
Lesson 3.1: Overview

THE CALENDAR
Lesson 3.1: Overview

1 ▪ Accessing the Calendar

The **Calendar** is a tool that allows you to organise your time. Three types of activity are managed by the Calendar: appointments, events and meetings. All these activities can be referred to as **items**.

Along with these three types of item, you can create a list of tasks you have to do.

▪ In the **Outlook** bar, click the **Outlook Shortcuts** group and click the **Calendar** folder.

You can also click the **Calendar** folder in the folder list.

Unless the setting is changed, the Calendar is shown in the **Day/Week/Month** view:

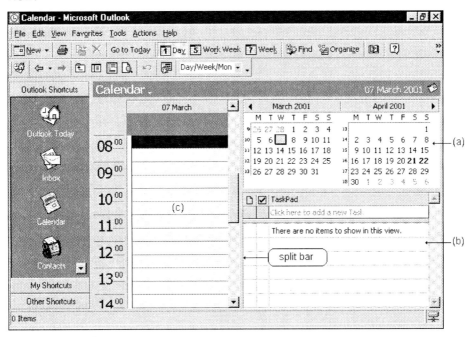

This view is made up of three panes: the **Date Navigator** (a), the **Task List** (b) and a one-day **Diary** (c) that shows the different activities planned for the day.

You can change the amount of space allocated to the Diary by dragging the split bar on the right of the Diary pane.

▣2 ▪ Activating a standard view

*The views enable you to see the **Calendar** folder in different ways.*

▪ Use **View - Current View** or open the list on the **Current View** tool `Day/Week/Mon ▾`.

▪ Click the option corresponding to one of the following views:

Day/Week/ Month	to see a list of appointments, events and meetings arranged for one or more days, several weeks or a specific month. This view includes a task list and is shown in the form of a diary or desk planner.
Day/Week/ Month View with AutoPreview	to see a list of appointments, events and meetings planned for one day.
Active Appointments	to display a list of all the appointments and meetings planned from today onwards with accompanying details.
Events	to see a list of all the events planned and their details.
Annual events	for a list of all the events that happen once a year with their details.
Recurring Appointments	to see a list of recurring appointments and the accompanying details.
By Category	for a list of all the items in the Calendar grouped according to their categories, with accompanying details.

THE CALENDAR
Lesson 3.1: Overview

⁎ Choose the sort of **Day/Week/Month** view you want to see by clicking one of the following tools:

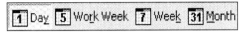

▣3 ▪ **Showing another date**

⁎ To move from month to month, use the arrowheads you can see in the top part of the date navigator.

⁎ If you want to jump to a month quickly, click the name of the active month in the date navigator and, holding the mouse button down, point to the month you want to see. If the month you want is not in the list, display it by dragging the mouse pointer up or down outside the list.

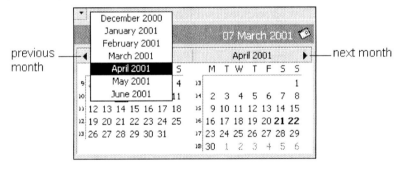

⁎ Release the mouse button and click the date you want to see.

⁎ **View - Go To - Go To Date** or Ctrl **G**

⁎ Type the **Date** you want in the corresponding text box or open the list and select the date.

⁎ Open the **Show in** list and select how the Diary should be shown: **Day Calendar**, **Week Calendar**, **Month Calendar** or **Work Week Calendar** and click **OK**.

*Return to today using **View - Go To - Go To Today** or click the **Go to Today** button on the **Standard** toolbar.*

⊞4 ▪ Customising the current view

Viewing by Month

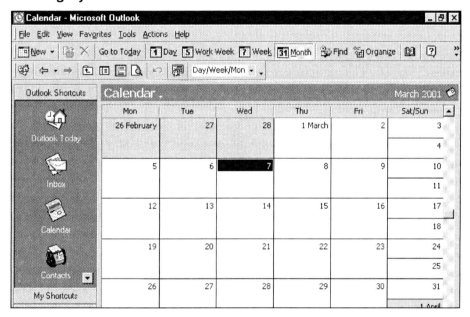

*In **Month** view only the Diary pane appears on the screen and alternate months appear with grey backgrounds. In this screen illustration the weekends are reduced (Saturdays and Sundays are shown in one column).*

▪ **View - Current View - Customize Current View**

▪ Click the **Other Settings** tab.

▪ If you want to display Saturdays and Sundays in the same way as other days (one day per column), deactivate the **Compress weekend days** option in the **Month** frame.

* To show appointment times as clocks, activate the **Show time as clocks** option in the **Month** frame.

* If you want to display the estimated end of an appointment, activate the **Show end time** option in the **Month** frame.

  *Bear in mind that, even if **Show end time** is selected, the estimated end time of appointments is not shown if you have activated the **Show time as clocks** option.*

* Click **OK** twice.

 In this view you can go to the first day in the month using Alt PgUp *and the last using* Alt PgDn.

Viewing by Week

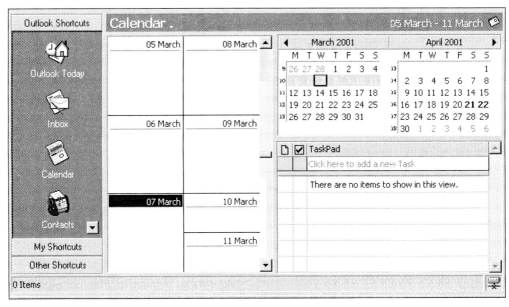

* **View - Current View - Customize Current View**
* Click the **Other Settings** button.

▪ To show appointment times as clocks, activate the **Show time as clocks** option in the **Week** frame. If you want to display the estimated end of an appointment, activate the **Show end time** option in the **Week** frame.

▪ Click **OK** twice.

Viewing one or more days

▪ To choose the days you want to display, select them in the Date Navigator. Select adjacent days by holding the Shift key down as you click and non-adjacent days by holding the Ctrl key down as you click.

You can also click the 1 Day *tool to display one day.*

On this screen the 7, 14 and 21 March 2001 have been selected in the Date Navigator.

❋ Use the following shortcut keys to change the number of days displayed:

Display 1 to 9 days   `Alt` + n on the alphanumerical keyboard where n is the number of days you want to display.

Display 10 days   `Alt` **0** (alphanumerical keyboard)

Display the week   `Alt` - (number pad)

Display the month   `Alt` =

❋ To change the timescale use **View - Current View - Customize Current View** and click the **Other Settings** button.

❋ Open the **Time scale** list in the **Day** frame and click the option that corresponds to the timescale you want. Click **OK** twice.

Below you can see **Practice exercise 3.1**. This exercise is made up of 4 steps. If you do not know how to complete one of the steps, go back to the lesson to refer to the corresponding title. When you have finished, check your work by reading the **Solution** on the next page.

Steps that are likely to be tested on the exam are marked with a ⊞ symbol. It is however recommended that you follow the whole exercise in order to gain a complete understanding of the lesson.

 Practice exercise 3.1

1. Select the **Calendar** and view its contents.

⊞ 2. Change the view in the **Calendar** so that you can see a list of all the items grouped by category.

   Now, return to the **Day/Week/Month** view in the **Calendar** folder.

⊞ 3. Go to the third month after the current month and select the **15th** of the month.

   Now return to today.

⊞ 4. Customise the **Month** view so that Saturdays and Sundays are shown in the same way as other days (one day per column).

   Activate **Month** view to see the result then return to **Day** view.

If you want to put what you have learned into practice in a real document, you can work on the summary exercise 3 for THE CALENDAR section that you can find at the end of this book.

It is often possible to perform a task in several different ways, but here only the quickest solution is presented. Go back to the lesson to see the other techniques that can be used.

 Solution to exercise 3.1

1. Go to the **Outlook Shortcuts** group by clicking the corresponding button on the **Outlook** bar then click the **Calendar** folder.

2. To change the view in the Calendar to show a list of all the items grouped by category, open the **View - Current View** menu and click the **By Category** option. Return to **Day/Week/Month** view by using **View - Current View** and clicking the **Day/Week/Month** option.

3. Show the third month after the current month by clicking the ▶ tool in the top right corner of the Date Navigator three times. Now, in the Date Navigator, click on the number **15** of the month in question. Return to today by clicking the **Go to Today** tool on the **Standard** toolbar.

4. Use **View - Current View - Customize Current View** and click the **Other Settings** button to customise the Month view. Deactivate the **Compress weekends** option in the **Month** frame and click **OK** twice. Activate the **Month** view to see the result by clicking the 31 Month tool.

   Return to the **Day** view by clicking 1 Day.

THE CALENDAR
Lesson 3.2: Calendar items

THE CALENDAR

Lesson 3.2: Calendar items

▤1 ▪ Creating an appointment

*An **appointment** is any activity for which you want to set aside time in the calendar without requiring the presence of other people or any extra resources.*

▪ Open the **Calendar** and use one of the following techniques:

- **File - New - Appointment** or ⌨Ctrl⌨Shift **A**

- **Actions - New Appointment** or ⌨Ctrl **N**

- Click the ▤New ▾ button.

*The word **Appointment** appears on the title bar of the window that opens.*

▪ Give the appointment a description in the **Subject** text box.

▪ Give the **Location** of the appointment either by typing it or selecting it from the corresponding list.

▪ Use the lists associated with the **Start time** option to indicate the starting date and time of the appointment. Give the end date and time using the lists associated with the **End time** option.

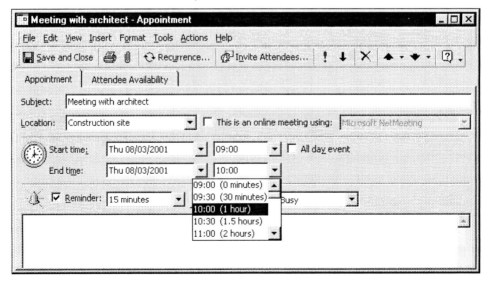

*Appointments have a default duration of half an hour. To make it easier to choose the **End time**, Outlook calculates the duration from the **Start time** you entered.*

▪ Deactivate the **Reminder** option if you do not want to set an alarm to remind you of this appointment (see Setting an alarm later in this chapter).

▪ Enter any extra information in the big text box in the bottom part of the window.

▪ Click the [🖫 Save and Close] button.

The appointment appears in the Diary. In a day view, Outlook shows the start and end times of appointments and their locations:

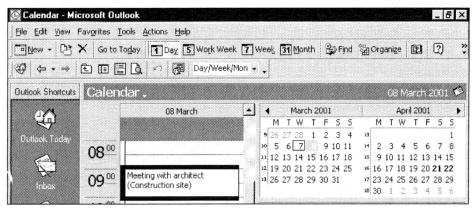

 *Double-click an appointment in the Diary to edit it. When you are creating an appointment, activate the **All day event** option to turn it into an event.*

You can also create an appointment by double-clicking a time slot in the Diary.

📖2 ▪ **Creating an event**

An **event** *is an activity that lasts at least 24 hours. It does not have a time slot in the Diary.*

▪ In the **Outlook** bar, click the **Outlook Shortcuts** group then the **Calendar** folder.

▪ If necessary, go to the first day of the event.

▪ **Actions - New All Day Event**

*The word **Event** appears on the title bar of the window that opens.*

▪ Type a description of the event in the **Subject** text box.

▪ Indicate the **Location** of the event either by typing it or select one from the drop-down list.

▪ If necessary, select a **Start time** for the event from the corresponding list.

▪ If necessary, select an **End time** for the event from the corresponding list.

▪ Make sure the **All day event** option is active.

▪ Deactivate the **Reminder** option if you do not want to set an alarm for this event (see Setting an alarm later in this chapter).

▪ Click 🖫 <u>S</u>ave and Close .

In the Diary, events are shown as headings giving the subject and location:

Calendar ▾		13 March 2001
13 March ▲	◀ March 2001	April 2001 ▶
Moving offices (New offices (South Gyle))	M T W T F S S	M T W T F S S
	9 26 27 28 1 2 3 4	13 1
08⁰⁰	10 5 6 [7] 8 9 10 11	14 2 3 4 5 6 7 8
	11 12 14 15 16 17 18	15 9 10 11 12 13 14 15
	12 19 20 21 22 23 24 25	16 16 17 18 19 20 **21 22**
09⁰⁰	13 26 27 28 29 30 31	17 23 24 25 26 27 28 29
		18 30 1 2 3 4 5 6

Edit an event by double-clicking it in the Diary pane.

*While you are creating an event, deactivate the **All day event** option to turn it into an appointment.*

 *Double-clicking the heading area of the Diary pane opens the **Event** window.*

3 ▪ Setting an alarm

This alarm is there to remind you about an appointment or an event.

▪ While you are creating or editing an item, make sure the **Reminder** option is active.

▪ In the following list, specify how long before the item (appointment, event or meeting) you want the alarm to go off.

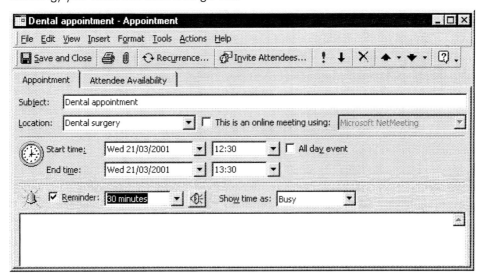

* You can customise the sound played when the alarm goes off by clicking the  button. Click the **Browse** button and select the sound file you want to play. If you do not want to hear a sound with the alarm, deactivate the **Play this sound** option. Click **OK** to confirm your choice.

* Click ⊞ Save and Close .

In day and week views, items for which you have set an alarm are marked with this symbol: ⧖.

⊟ *You can deactivate*

⊟ *an alarm while you are creating or editing an item by deactivating the **Reminder** option.*

*By default, while you are creating an appointment, the **Reminder** is active and the alarm is set for 15 minutes before the start of the appointment. Deactivate this default option or change the time the alarm goes off using **Tools - Options - Preferences** tab.*

⊞4 ▪ Responding to an alarm

When an alarm goes off, Outlook shows a dialog box reminding you of the subject and location of the item:

* To repeat the alarm, indicate when you want to repeat it in the **Click Snooze to be reminded again** list then click the **Snooze** button.

* Click **Dismiss** if you want to close the alarm.

* You can consult the item in question by clicking the **Open Item** button. When you have finished, close the window by clicking ☒.

🖳5 ▪ Creating a recurring item

You can set an appointment, event or meeting to repeat automatically at regular intervals.

* You need to be creating or editing the item in question.

* **Actions - Recurrence** or ⟳ Recurrence... or ⌨Ctrl **G**

* If need be, change the **Start** and/or **End** times for the item using the lists in the **Appointment time** frame.

* Use the different options in the **Recurrence pattern** to define when and how often the item should be repeated.

* Indicate how long the recurrence is to last using the following options in the **Range of recurrence** frame:

No end date	the recurring item is repeated indefinitely.
End after n occurrences	the recurring item is repeated for the number of times given in the text box.
End by	the recurrence ends on the date given in the text box.

* If necessary, specify the **Start** date for the item in the corresponding list in the **Range of recurrence** frame.

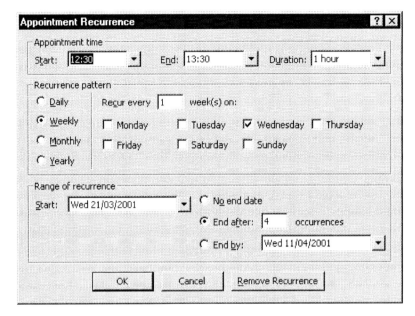

In this example the appointment will recur every Friday from the 08/03/2001 from 12:30 to 13:30 for a duration of four weeks.

※ Click **OK** then ▣ Save and Close .

📑 *When you want to open a recurring item, Outlook asks you if you want to open the selected item or all its occurrences:*

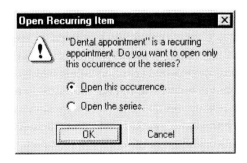

*If you only want to view recurring appointments, use **View - Current View - Recurring Appointments.***

*You can remove an item's recurrence by double-clicking one of the items. Make sure the **Open this occurrence** option is active and click **OK**. Now use **Action - Recurrence**, click the **Remove Recurrence** button then click*

 *You can create a recurring item (appointment or meeting) by activating the corresponding option in the **Actions** menu.*

6 ▪ Creating a meeting

*A **meeting** is an appointment that requires the presence of several people and makes use of resources.*

▪ In the **Outlook** bar, click the **Outlook Shortcuts** group and choose the **Calendar** folder.

▪ If necessary, select the day and time the meeting should start, or the corresponding time slot.

▪ **Actions - Plan a Meeting** or

By default, the meeting organiser is the only participant.

▪ Now add all the meeting attendees and any resources:

- click the **Invite Others** button,

- for each participant, select the address book that contains their name in the **Show Names from the** list, select their name and click 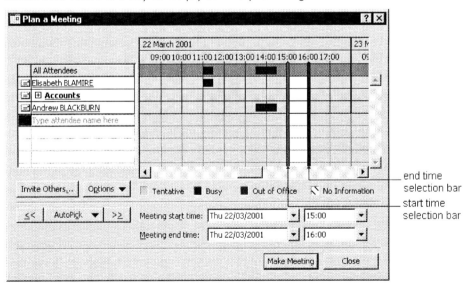 Required -> if their presence is obligatory or Optional -> if their presence is optional; for each resource, select its name and click Resources -> (you need the appropriate permissions to invite and schedule resources).

A resource is a material item (such as a conference room or an overhead projector) represented on your network by a mailbox managed by an administrator. When you are working with Microsoft Exchange Server, this person can schedule and configure resources to accept or refuse meetings according to their availability.

❋ Confirm your choices by clicking **OK**.

The participants' names appear in the dialog box. The envelope symbol you can see at the left of the names indicates that a meeting request will be sent. The grid in the right of the dialog box shows the availability of the meeting attendees and resources. There is a key to help you interpret the grid.

* If necessary, define the starting and finishing time of the meeting using the lists associated with the **Start time** and **End time** options or by dragging the meeting selection bars in the grid.

*The **AutoPick** button displays options for choosing the next available time slot for each participant automatically.*

*The ⊟ icon you can see at the left of a participant's name indicates that they will receive a meeting invitation. If you do not want a participant to receive an invitation, click the icon and choose the **Don't send meeting to this attendee** option.*

* If you want to expand a distribution list to see each of its members, click the plus sign (+) that precedes the list.

A distribution list contains several members: when you send a message to a distribution list, you are sending it to all the list members at once (see Creating a distribution list - Chapter 4.1 Contacts).

Click **OK** when the message appears telling you that the list will be replaced by the addresses of its members and that you cannot undo this change.

The name of each member of the list appears preceded by the ⊟ symbol.

* Click the **Make Meeting** button.

*The word **Meeting** is shown on the title bar of the window that opens.*

* Enter the meeting's characteristics: its **Subject**, its **Location**, it recurrence and so on, as you would when creating an appointment.

* Click the ⊟ **Send** button to send the meeting invitation.

* Close the **Plan a Meeting** window by clicking the **Close** button.

In a day or week view, meeting items contain this symbol ⊡.

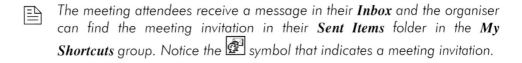 *The meeting attendees receive a message in their **Inbox** and the organiser can find the meeting invitation in their **Sent Items** folder in the **My Shortcuts** group. Notice the ⊡ symbol that indicates a meeting invitation.*

7 ▪ Adding/removing attendees from a meeting

* Double-click the meeting in question.

* If the meeting is a recurring one, choose whether all the meetings are concerned (**Open the series**) or just the selected one (**Open this occurrence**) then click **OK**.

* **Actions - Add or Remove Attendees**

  The **Select Attendees and Resources** dialog box re-opens.

* Cancel a participant's invitation by clicking his/her name in the **Required**, **Optional** or **Resources** box and pressing Del.

* To invite more people (or resources), select them in the address list and add them to the **Required**, **Optional** or **Resources** list by clicking the corresponding button.

* Click **OK**.

* Click Save and Close.

* Choose what sort of update you want to send to the participants by activating one of the options then click **OK**.

You can add invitations by opening the meeting, clicking the **Attendee Availability** tab then clicking the **Invite Others** button.

8 ▪ **Replying to a meeting request**

▪ Select the **Calendar** folder and double-click the item or select the **Inbox** folder and double-click the message that contains the meeting invitation.

▪ Reply to the meeting request by clicking ✔ Accept if you want to accept the invitation, ? Tentative if you can provisionally accept the invitation or ✘ Decline if you want to turn down the invitation.

A dialog box opens.

▪ Choose one of the following options:

Edit the response before sending	to add a comment to your reply.
Send the response now	to send the reply without a comment.
Don't send a response	if you do not want to reply to the request.

▪ If you have chosen to add a comment to your reply, type the text then click Send.

When you accept or tentatively accept a meeting invitation, Outlook places the meeting in your Calendar.

In your **Sent Item** *folder, the subject of the reply you have sent is preceded by* **Accepted, Refused** *or* **Tentative**.

 The meeting organiser (who sent the invitations) can see a summary of the replies for the meeting by opening the meeting concerned and clicking the **Attendee Availability** *tab.*

9 ▪ Managing items

※ To edit a calendar item, double-click the item you want to modify. Make the appropriate changes then click the 💾 Save and Close button.

> 📄 *If you only want to change the item's subject, simply click the item once and edit the subject directly. Confirm by pressing* ↵.

※ To delete items, select them (Ctrl -click to select several items at once) then use **Edit - Delete** or ✕ or Ctrl **D**

When you delete a recurring item, Outlook asks if you want to delete the selected item only or the whole series.

※ Delete all the occurrences by choosing the appropriate option or choose **Delete this one** to delete the selected item then click **OK**.

※ To move an item, start by positioning the mouse pointer to the left of the item you want to move. When the pointer takes this shape: ┿, drag the item to a new time (Diary pane) or date (Date Navigator).

> 📄 *Hold down the* Ctrl *key while you are dragging if you want to copy the item.*

Below you can see **Practice exercise 3.2**. This exercise is made up of 9 steps. If you do not know how to complete one of the steps, go back to the lesson to refer to the corresponding title. When you have finished, check your work by reading the **Solution** on the next page.

Steps that are likely to be tested on the exam are marked with a symbol. It is however recommended that you follow the whole exercice in order to gain a complete understanding of the lesson.

👉 Practice exercise 3.2

1. Create an appointment scheduled one week from today's date. The details of the appointment are as follows:

- the subject of the appointment is **Meeting with architect**.
- the appointment will take place at the **Construction site**.
- it will begin at **09:00** and end at **10:00**.
- you do not need a reminder for this appointment.

2. Create an event for the following **Monday** and **Tuesday**:

- the event is called **Moving offices**.
- the event will take place at the **New offices (South Gyle)**.
- you do not need to program an alarm to remind you about this event.

3. Create an appointment, **45 minutes** from now:

- the appointment's subject is **Dental appointment**.
- the appointment's location is the **Dental surgery**.
- the appointment is to last **1 hour**.
- a dialog box reminding you of the appointment should appear **30 minutes** before the appointment's start time.

4. Wait for the alarm for the appointment you created in step 3 and, when it appears, read the contents of the **Reminder** dialog box before deactivating the alarm.

5. Create a recurring appointment which you should program for the second working day each month for four months, starting next month. The appointment should contain this information:

   - the recurring appointment's subject is **Project meeting**.
   - its location is the **Heriot Room**.
   - the appointment should begin at **14:00** and end at **15:30**.
   - a reminder should appear for this appointment **20 minutes** before the start time.

6. Create a meeting for the first **Thursday** of next month and invite two people (one whose presence is required and the other whose presence is optional). The meeting should contain this information:

   - it should begin at **15:00** and end at **16:00**.
   - the meeting subject is **Management committee**.
   - the meeting should take place in the **Crichton Room**.
   - a reminder dialog box should appear **30 minutes** before the meeting is due to start.

   If you are not able to invite two people to a meeting, you cannot complete this step.

7. Add another person to the meeting you created in step 6. This new participant is required to be at the meeting and all the participants should receive an update.

   You can only complete this step if you have previously completed step 6.

8. Now you should create a meeting on another computer. Plan this meeting a week from now and invite yourself (your presence is required) and another person, whose presence is optional. The meeting should include the following information:

- it is to start at **11:00** and end at **11:30**.

- the meeting's subject is **Half-year report**.

- the meeting is to take place in the **Vogrie Room**.

- a reminder dialog box should appear **10 minutes** before the meeting is due to start.

Once you have sent the meeting invitations, go back to your own computer.

If you are not able to use another computer, you cannot complete this step.

Give a positive reply to the meeting request you have just created at another computer and send it without adding a comment.

9. Change the **Meeting with architect** appointment you created for a week from today as follows: <u>Start time</u>: **13:30** and <u>End time</u>: **15:00**

Move the appointment called **Project meeting** that you had planned for the second working day of each month so that the start time is **14:30** and not 14:00.

If you want to put what you have learned into practice in a real document, you can work on the summary exercise 3 for THE CALENDAR section that you can find at the end of this book.

It is often possible to perform a task in several different ways, but here only the quickest solution is presented. Go back to the lesson to see the other techniques that can be used.

Solution to exercise 3.2

1. To create an appointment seven days from today with the information given in step 1, activate the **Calendar** and use **Actions - New Appointment**.

   Click in the **Subject** box and type **Meeting with architect**. Click in the **Location** text box and type **Construction site**.

   Open the first list associated with the **Start time** option and select the date that is seven days from today. Now open the second list associated with the **Start time** option and click **09:00**.

   If necessary, open the first list associated with the **End time** option and select the date that is seven days from now. Open the second **End time** list and choose **10:30 (1.5 hours)**.

   Deactivate the **Reminder** option and click <kbd>Save and Close</kbd> to create the appointment.

2. To create an event programmed for the following Monday and Tuesday as shown in step 2 of the exercise, make sure you are in the **Calendar** folder in the **Outlook Shortcuts** groups and use **Actions - New All Day Event**.

   Click in the **Subject** text box and type **Moving offices**. Click in the **Location** text box and type **New offices (South Gyle)**.

   Open the **Start time** list and choose next **Monday**. Open the **End time** list and choose next **Tuesday**.

   Make sure the **Reminder** option is deactivated and create the event by clicking <kbd>Save and Close</kbd>.

3. To create an appointment scheduled for 45 minutes from now as instructed in step 3, go into the **Outlook Shortcuts** group's **Calendar** folder and click [□ New ▾].

In the **Subject** text box type **Dental appointment**. Click in the **Location** text box and type **Dental surgery**.

Open the first **Start time** list and make sure that today's date is selected. In the second **Start time** list, either type or select the time of the appointment, which should be **45 minutes** from now.

Now, if necessary, open the first **End time** list and select today's date. In the second **End time** list, type or select the finishing time for the appointment, which is to last **1 hour**.

Make sure the **Reminder** option is active then open the associated list and choose **30 minutes**.

Create the appointment by clicking [🖫 Save and Close].

4. When the **Reminder** dialog box appears, read its contents then deactivate the alarm by clicking **Dismiss**.

5. To create a recurring appointment to be scheduled for every second working day of the month, starting next month and to run for four months, go to the **Calendar** folder in the **Outlook Shortcuts** group and click [□ New ▾].

Click the [↻ Recurrence...] button.

Open the **Start** list in the **Appointment time** frame and choose **14:00**. Open the **End** list in the same frame and choose **15:30 (1.5 hours)**.

Now activate the **Monthly** option in the **Recurrence pattern** frame then the **The** option. Choose **second** in the first drop-down list after the **The** option then choose **weekday** in the second list. Make sure that **1** is the value in the **of every n month(s)** box.

Open the **Start** list in the **Range of recurrence** frame and choose the date that corresponds to the second working day of next month.

In the **End after n occurrences** text box of the **Range of recurrence** frame, type **4** then click **OK**.

Now click in the **Subject** text box and type **Project meeting** then type **Heriot Room** in the **Location** text box.

Make sure the **Reminder** is active and type **20 minutes** in the associated text box.

Finish by clicking [Save and Close] to create the recurring appointment.

6. To create a meeting planned for the first Thursday of next month, and invite two people (one required, the other optional), first make sure that you are in the **Calendar** folder in the **Outlook Shortcuts** group then use **Actions - Plan a Meeting**.

Choose the participants by clicking the **Invite Others** button then open the **Show Names from the** list and choose the address book you want to use.

Select the name of the required participant and click the [Required ->] button. Now select the name of the person whose presence is optional and click the [Optional ->] button. Confirm your choices by clicking **OK**.

Open the first **Start time** list and choose the date of the first Thursday of next month. Now open the second **Start time** list and choose **15:00**.

If necessary, open the first **End time** list and choose the date of the first Thursday of next month then open the second **End time** and pick **16:00**.

Click the **Make Meeting** button.

Now click in the **Subject** text box and type **Management committee** then click in the **Location** text box and type **Crichton Room**.

Check that the **Reminder** option is active and choose **30 minutes** from the list.

Send the meeting request to the participants by clicking [≡ Send] then close the **Plan a Meeting** window.

7. To add a participant to the meeting created in step 6, make sure that you are, in the **Calendar** folder (**Outlook Shortcuts** group) then, in the Date Navigator, click the date of the first Thursday next month. Double-click the **Management committee** meeting and use **Actions - Add or Remove Attendees**.

Open the **Show Names from the** list and choose the address book you want. Select the participant's name and click [Required ->]. Confirm by clicking **OK**.

Click [Save and Close], activate the **Send updates to all attendees** option and click **OK**.

8. To use a different computer to create a meeting as described in step 8 of the exercise, first go to another computer. Make sure you are in the **Calendar** folder (**Outlook Shortcuts** group) then use **Actions - Plan a Meeting**.

Choose the participants by clicking the **Invite Others** button then open the **Show Names from the** list and choose the address book you want to use. Select your name and click the [Required ->] button. Now select the name of the person whose presence is optional and click the [Optional ->] button. Confirm your choices by clicking **OK**.

Open the first **Start time** list and choose the date of the first Thursday of next month. Now open the second **Start time** list and choose **11:00**.

If necessary, open the first **End time** list and choose the date of the first Thursday of next month then open the second **End time** list and pick **11:30**.

Click the **Make Meeting** button.

Now click in the **Subject** text box and type **Half-year report** then in the **Location** text box and type **Vogrie Room**.

Check that the **Reminder** option is active and select **10 minutes** from the list.

Send the meeting request to the participants by clicking ⌐⊐ Send then close the **Plan a Meeting** window.

Now, to send a positive reply to the meeting request you have just sent yourself, go back to you computer and open your **Inbox**. Double-click the **Half-year report** message. Click the ✔ Accept button, activate the **Send the response now** choice and click **OK**.

9. To change the start and end times of the appointment you have made for one week from today called "Meeting with architect", go to the **Calendar** folder (**Outlook Shortcuts** group). In the Date Navigator, click the day that is a week from now and double-click the **Meeting with architect** appointment.

Open the second **Start time** list and select **13:30**. Open the second **End time** list and choose **15:00 (1.5 hours)**.

Click 🖫 Save and Close to save the changes you have made to this appointment.

Now move the "Project meeting" appointment programmed for the second working day of the following month to 14:30. Click in the Date Navigator on the day in question and, in the Diary, place the mouse pointer to the left of the **Project meeting** item. When the mouse pointer takes this shape ✛, drag the appointment downwards until its start time is **14:30**.

THE CALENDAR
Lesson 3.3: Printing and saving

1 ▪ Printing the Calendar

▪ In the **Outlook** bar, click the **Outlook Shortcuts** group then the **Calendar** folder.

▪ If necessary, activate the **Day/Week/Month** view using **View - Current View - Day/Week/Month**.

▪ **File - Print** or 🖨 or ⌨Ctrl **P**

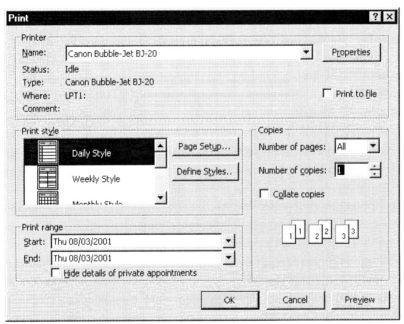

▪ Select the **Print style** you want from the corresponding list:

Daily Style	prints one day per page with areas for tasks and notes.
Weekly Style	prints one week per page without tasks or notes.
Monthly Style	prints one month per page without tasks or notes.

Tri-fold Style prints a day, month and task list on one page in three distinct sections, making it easy to fold the page into a leaflet.

Calendar Details Style prints details of the Calendar items as a list.

※ Indicate the dates you want to print from the Calendar using the **Start** and **End** lists in the **Print range** frame: the **Print style** you choose determines how many days are to be printed (for example, choosing the **Monthly Style** will print the month that corresponds to the selected date).

※ In the **Number of pages** list of the **Copies** frame, choose whether you want to print even or odd numbered pages or both.

※ Type the number of copies you want to print in the **Number of copies** text box in the **Copies** frame.

※ Activate the **Collate copies** option if you want the pages to be printed copy by copy and not page by page.

※ Click **OK** to start printing or choose to see a **Preview** by clicking the corresponding button.

> *Each print style can be customised temporarily by clicking the **Page Setup** button or permanently using the **Define Styles** button in the **Print** dialog box (**File - Print**).*
>
> *The* *button will display a print preview.*

🖥2 ▪ Printing Calendar items

※ Select the items you want to print, holding the ⌈Ctrl⌉ key down as you click to select several items.

※ **File - Print** or 🖨 or ⌈Ctrl⌉ **P**

※ Select the **Memo Style** option in the **Print style** frame.

- If you have selected several items, indicate whether you want to **Start each item on a new page** by activating this option in the **Print options** frame.

- To print any attachments with the items, activate **Print attached files with item(s)** option in the **Print options** frame.

- Choose to print odd and/or even pages using the **Number of pages** list in the **Copies** frame.

- Enter how many copies you want to print in the **Number of copies** box in the **Copies** frame.

- To print copy by copy and not page by page, activate the **Collate copies** option.

- Click **OK** to start printing.

❑3 ▪ Defining page setup characteristics for each print style

For the Daily Style

- Go into the **Calendar** and use **File - Page Setup - Daily Style**.

- Click the **Format** tab.

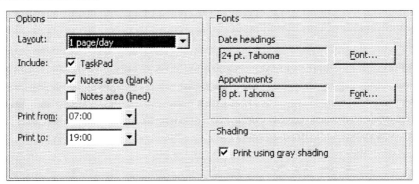

- Open the **Layout** list in the **Options** frame and select one of the following choices:

1 page/day   to print the Diary, notes and task list on one page.

2 pages/day   to print the Diary on one page and the task list and notes on another.

» Activate or deactivate the **TaskPad** option in the **Options** frame, depending on whether or not you want to print the task list.

» Activate or deactivate the **Notes area (blank)** option in the **Options** frame on whether you want to include a blank (unlined) section for notes.

» Activate or deactivate the **Notes area (lined)** option in the **Options** frame on whether you want to include a lined section for notes.

» Indicate the period you want to print using the **Print from** and **Print to** lists in the **Options** frame.

» Change the font used for headings by clicking the **Font** button under the **Date headings** option in the **Fonts** frame.

» Change the font used for the text by clicking the **Font** button under **Appointments** in the **Fonts** frame.

» If you do not want light grey shading for the headings, dates and other items, deactivate the **Print using gray shading** option in the **Shading** frame.

» Click **OK**.

For the Weekly Style

» Go into **Calendar** and use **File - Page Setup - Weekly Style**.

» Click the **Format** tab.

```
┌─ Options ──────────────────────────────┐  ┌─ Fonts ─────────────────────────────┐
│  Arrange      ⦿ Top to bottom          │  │  Date headings                      │
│               ○ Left to right          │  │  ┌──────────────────┐  ┌─────────┐  │
│                                        │  │  │24 pt. Tahoma     │  │ Font... │  │
│  Layout:      │1 page/week      ▼│     │  │  └──────────────────┘  └─────────┘  │
│                                        │  │  Appointments                       │
│  Include:     ☐ Notes area (blank)     │  │  ┌──────────────────┐  ┌─────────┐  │
│  ☐ TaskPad    ☐ Notes area (lined)     │  │  │8 pt. Tahoma      │  │ Font... │  │
│                                        │  │  └──────────────────┘  └─────────┘  │
│  Print from:  │07:00        ▼│         │  └─────────────────────────────────────┘
│                                        │  ┌─ Shading ───────────────────────────┐
│  Print to:    │19:00        ▼│         │  │  ☑ Print using gray shading         │
│  ☐ Don't Print Weekends                │  │                                     │
└────────────────────────────────────────┘  └─────────────────────────────────────┘
```

» Activate one of the following choices in the **Options** frame depending on how you want to display the days:

Top to bottom the days will be placed in two columns: Monday will be at the top of the left column and Sunday at the bottom of the right column.

Left to right the days will be shown in a grid in which the dates occupy the columns and the times the rows.

» Open the **Layout** list in the **Options** frame and choose one of the following:

1 page/week to print one week on one page.

2 pages/week to print one week on two pages: Monday, Tuesday and Wednesday are printed on one page and Thursday, Friday, Saturday and Sunday are printed on the second page.

» Activate or deactivate the **Notes area (blank)** option in the **Options** depending on whether you want to include a blank (unlined) section for notes.

» Activate or deactivate the **Notes area (lined)** option in the **Options** depending on whether you want to include a lined section for notes.

» Activate or deactivate the **TaskPad** option in the **Options** frame, depending on whether or not you want to print the task list.

» If you have chosen the **Left to right** option, you can choose the start and end of the period you want to print using the **Print from** and **Print to** lists in the **Options** frame.

- If you have chosen the **Left to right** option, you can choose to exclude Saturday and Sunday from the print range by activating the **Don't Print Weekends** option.

- Change the font used for headings by clicking the **Font** button under the **Date headings** option in the **Fonts** frame.

- Change the font used for the text by clicking the **Font** button under **Appointments** in the **Fonts** frame.

- If you do not want light grey shading for the headings, dates and other items, deactivate the **Print using gray shading** option in the **Shading** frame.

- Click **OK**.

For the Monthly Style

- Go into the **Calendar** and use **File - Page Setup - Monthly Style**.

- Click the **Format** tab.

- Open the **Layout** list in the **Options** frame and choose one of the following choices:

    1 page/month   to print a month on one page.

    2 pages/month   to print a month on two pages.

- Activate or deactivate the **TaskPad** option in the **Options** frame, depending on whether or not you want to print the task list.

- Activate or deactivate the **Notes area (blank)** option in the **Options** depending on whether you want to include a blank (unlined) section for notes.

- Activate or deactivate the **Notes area (lined)** option in the **Options** depending on whether you want to include a lined section for notes.

- If you want to exclude Saturdays and Sundays from the print range, activate the **Don't Print Weekends** option.

- If you do not mind that a page contains days from two different months, deactivate the **Print Exactly One Month Per Page** option.

※ Change the font used for headings by clicking the **Font** button under the **Date headings** option in the **Fonts** frame.

※ Change the font used for the text by clicking the **Font** button under **Appointments** in the **Fonts** frame.

※ If you do not want light grey shading for the headings, dates and other items, deactivate the **Print using gray shading** option in the **Shading** frame.

※ Click **OK**.

For the Tri-fold Style

※ Go into the **Calendar** and use **File - Page Setup - Tri-fold Style**.

※ Click the **Format** tab.

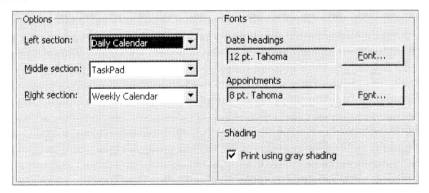

※ Choose what information you want to print on each page of the leaflet using the **Left section** (left column of the page), **Middle section** (middle column of the page) and **Right section** (right column of the page) lists:

Daily Calendar   prints one day per page.

Weekly Calendar   prints one week per page.

Monthly Calendar   prints one month per page.

TaskPad   prints the task list.

Notes (Blank)   prints an unlined area for notes.

Notes (Lined)   prints a lined area for notes.

* Change the font used for headings by clicking the **Font** button under **Date headings** option in the **Fonts** frame.

* Change the font used for the text by clicking the **Font** button under **Appointments** in the **Fonts** frame.

* If you do not want light grey shading for the headings, dates and other items, deactivate the **Print using gray shading** option in the **Shading** frame.

* Click **OK**.

For the Details Style

* Go into the **Calendar** and use **File - Page Setup - Calendar Details Style**.

* Click the **Format** tab.

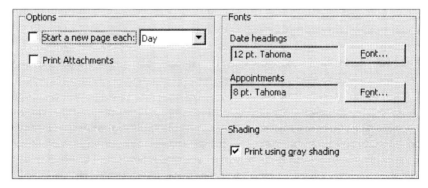

* If you want to print per **Day**, per **Week** or per **Month**, activate the **Start a new page each** option and select the appropriate choice from the associated list.

* Activate **Print Attachments** if you want to print all the attachments with items.

* Change the font used for headings by clicking the **Font** button under the **Date headings** option in the **Fonts** frame.

* Change the font used for the text by clicking the **Font** button under **Appointments** in the **Fonts** frame.

» If you do not want light grey shading for the headings, dates and other items, deactivate the **Print using gray shading** option in the **Shading** frame.

» Click **OK**.

For the Memo Style

» Go into the **Calendar** and use **File - Page Setup - Memo Style**.

» Click the **Format** tab.

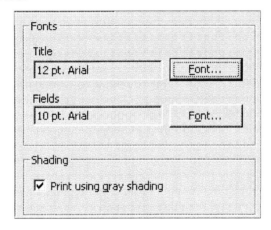

» Change the font used for headings and headers by clicking **Font** button under the **Title** option in the **Fonts** frame.

» Change the font used for the text by clicking the **Font** button for the **Fields** in the **Fonts** frame.

» If you do not want light grey shading for the headings, dates and other items, deactivate the **Print using gray shading** option in the **Shading** frame then click **OK**.

You can view a ***Print Preview*** *for each page setup so that you can see the effect of the options you have chosen in the* ***Page Setup*** *dialog box. To do this, click the button in the* ***Page Setup*** *dialog box. You can return to the* ***Page Setup*** *dialog box by clicking the* 📖 Page Setup... *button in the print preview window.*

The ***Print*** *button in the* ***Page Setup*** *dialog box opens the* ***Print*** *dialog box so that you can define the print settings.*

 You can also define page setup options for a given print style by selecting the style in the ***Print style*** *list of the* ***Print*** *dialog box* ***(File - Print)*** *then clicking the* ***Page Setup*** *button.*

▣4 ▪ Defining the margins and/or the orientation for a print style

- ▪ Go into the **Calendar** and use the **File - Page Setup** command.
- ▪ Click the option that corresponds to the print style for which you want to define the margins and/or orientation.
- ▪ Click the **Paper** tab.

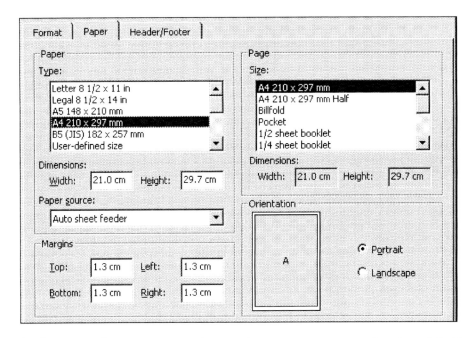

In the **Paper** frame you can choose the paper you are using to print. Use the **Page** frame to define the size and orientation of the page for the **Type** of paper you have selected in the **Paper** frame.

» For each margin you want to set, click in the corresponding text box (**Top**, **Bottom**, **Right** or **Left**) in the **Margins** frame and type the appropriate value in centimetres.

» Define the orientation by activating either **Portrait** or **Landscape** in the **Orientation** frame.

» Click **OK**.

You can also change the margins and/or orientation for a given print style by selecting the style in the **Print style** list of the **Print** dialog box **(File - Print)** then clicking the **Page Setup** button and the **Paper** tab.

5 ▪ Defining headers and footers for a print style

▪ Go into the **Calendar** and use **File - Page Setup**.

▪ Click the print style for which you want to define the headers and footers.

▪ Click the **Header/Footer** tab.

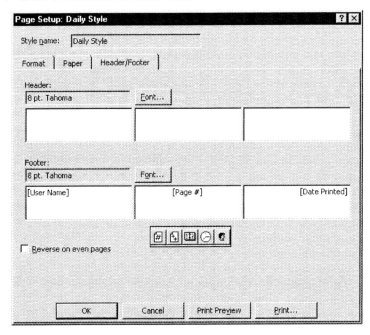

*By default, the user's name, page number and the day's date are printed in the left, centre and right sections of the **Footer** respectively.*

▪ For each header or footer you want to define:

- click in the text box that corresponds to the position of the text you are defining (left, centre or right for the **Header** or **Footer**).

- type the information you want to print, using the ↵ key to enter information on several lines.

- if necessary, you can use the following buttons to insert particular information:

inserts the page number.

inserts the total number of pages.

inserts today's date.

inserts the time of printing.

inserts the user's name.

- you can format the information you have typed by selecting it and clicking the **Font** button for the **Header** or **Footer** options, whichever is appropriate.

※ Activate the **Reverse on even pages** option if you want the contents of the header and footer sections printed on the left of an even-numbered page to be printed on the right of an odd-numbered page and vice vera.

※ Click **OK**.

*You can also change the margins and/or orientation for a given print style by selecting the style in the **Print style** list of the **Print** dialog box (**File - Print**) then clicking the **Page Setup** button and the **Header/Footer** tab.*

⊞6 ▪ Saving a calendar as a Web page

By saving your Calendar as a Web page on your company's intranet or your Internet site, you can share it with other users.

※ In the **Outlook** bar, click the **Outlook Shortcuts** group and choose the **Calendar** folder.

※ **File - Save as Web Page**

※ Select the **Start date** for the calendar in the **Duration** frame.

※ Open the **End date** list in the **Duration** frame and select the last date to appear in the calendar.

※ In the **Options** frame, activate the **Include appointment details** option if you want to include comments about the Calendar items in your Web page.

※ If you want to use a background picture in the Calendar, activate the **Use background graphic** option in the **Options** frame then click **Browse** to select it.

※ Fill in the **Calendar title** text box (the user's name appears by default) in the **Save as** frame.

※ In the **File name** text box type the folder or URL at which you want to save the Calendar or click the **Browse** button and select it.

※ Activate the **Open saved web page in browser** option if you want to start the browser and see the Web page as soon as it is saved.

THE CALENDAR

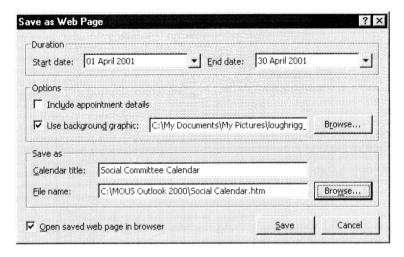

■ Click **Save**.

■ If necessary, close your browser window by clicking the ☒ button.

Below you can see **Practice exercise 3.3**. This exercise is made up of 6 steps. If you do not know how to complete one of the steps, go back to the lesson to refer to the corresponding title. When you have finished, check your work by reading the **Solution** on the next page.

All the steps in this exercise are likely to be tested in the exam.

 Practice exercise 3.3

1. Print two copies of your calendar for this week and next week.

2. Print the Calendar item called **Management committee**, planned for the first Thursday of the following month, and print the item scheduled for the second working day of next month called **Project meeting**. These two items should be printed on one page.

3. Define these page setup options for the **Weekly Style**:

    - the days on a page should be shown in a grid,

    - each week should be printed on one page,

    - you should include the task list and a blank area for notes,

    - define the time slot for the printed calendar as follows: starting at **8:00** and ending at **18:30**,

    - apply the **Arial** font, size **9** to the characters.

4. For the **Weekly Style** print style, set top, bottom, left and right margins of **1 cm** and choose the **Landscape** orientation.

5. First delete the default footers for the **Weekly Style** print style. Now create the headers and footers described below for this print style:

- the user's name should be printed in the top left corner of each page with **Bold** formatting,

- the page numbers should be printed at the bottom of each page, in the middle, as follows: **Page [Page #]/[Total pages]**,

- the date and time of printing are to be printed in the top right hand corner of each page as follows: **[Date Printed] at [Time Printed]**,

- now print the Calendar for the two weeks following this week.

6. Save Calendar for next month as a Web page following these instructions:

- the Web page should not include comments about Calendar items,

- choose any background picture you want for the Web page,

- the calendar should be called **Management Committee Calendar**,

- the calendar's file name is **Committee Calendar.htm** and it should be saved in the **MOUS Outlook 2000** folder,

- you want to see the Web page in your browser as soon as it has been saved.

After looking at the Web page, close your browser.

If you want to put what you have learned into practice in a real document, you can work on the Summary exercise 3 for THE CALENDAR section that you can find at the end of this book.

It is often possible to perform a task in several different ways, but here only the quickest solution is presented. Go back to the lesson to see the other techniques that can be used.

 Solution to exercise 3.3

1. To print two copies of the current week's and next week's calendar, open the **Outlook Shortcuts** group by clicking the corresponding button on the **Outlook** bar and click the **Calendar** folder. If necessary, activate **Day/Week/Month** view using **View - Current View - Day/Week/Month** then click the 🖨 tool. Select the **Weekly Style** from the **Print style** frame.

   Open the **Start** list in the **Print range** frame and select the date for the first day of this week. Now open the **End** list in the **Print range** frame and select the date of the last day of next week.

   Type **2** in the **Number of copies** text box then click **OK**.

2. To print the calendar item defined for the first Thursday of next month (with Management committee as the subject) and the item planned for the second working day of next month (whose subject is Project meeting), first make sure that the **Calendar** folder in the **Outlook Shortcuts** group is selected.

   In the Date Navigator, click on the date of the first Thursday of next month and, holding down the ⎡Ctrl⎦ key, click the date of the second working day of next month. Now, in the Diary, click the **Management committee** item and, holding down the ⎡Ctrl⎦ key, click the **Project meeting** item.

   Click the 🖨 tool and choose the **Memo Style** from the **Print style** frame.

So that both items will be printed on the same page, make sure the **Start each item on a new page** option in the **Print options** frame is deactivated.

Click **OK** to start printing.

3. To define the page setup options set out in step 3 of the exercise for the **Weekly Style** print style, first make sure that the **Calendar** folder (**Outlook Shortcuts** group) is selected, use **File - Page Setup - Weekly Style** then click the **Format** tab.

For the days to be shown in a grid on the page, activate the **Left to right** choice in the **Options** frame.

To ensure that each week is printed on one page, make sure the **1 page/week** choice is selected in the **Layout** list of the **Options** frame.

Include the task list and a blank space for notes by clicking the **TaskPad** and **Notes area (blank)** options in the **Options** frame.

To make the print range start at 8:00, open the **Print from** list and choose **08:00**. For the print range to end at 18:30, open the **Print to** list and choose **18:30**.

Now, to apply a size 9 Arial font to the characters, click the **Font** button for the **Appointments**. Choose **Arial** from the **Font** list and choose **9** in the **Size** list before clicking **OK**.

Click **OK** to confirm these page setup parameters.

4. To apply 1cm margins at the top, bottom, left and right of the page and choose a Landscape orientation for the Weekly Style, make sure that the **Calendar** folder (**Outlook Shortcuts** group) is selected, use **File - Page Setup - Weekly Style** and click the **Paper** tab.

Define the new margins by typing **1** in the **Top**, **Bottom**, **Left** and **Right** text boxes of the **Margins** frame.

Choose a Landscape orientation by activating the **Landscape** option in the **Orientation** frame.

Confirm your choices by clicking **OK**.

▦ 5. To remove all the default footers for the Weekly Style, first make sure that the **Calendar** folder in the **Outlook Shortcuts** group is selected, use **File - Page Setup - Weekly Style** then click the **Header/Footer** tab. Select [**User Name**] in the left section of the **Footer** and press ⌑Del⌑. Select [**Page #**] in the middle of the **Footer** and press ⌑Del⌑. Finally, select [**Date Printed**] in the right part of the **Footer** and press ⌑Del⌑.

Now, to print the user's name in the top left of the page, click in the left section of the **Header** then click the ⌑ button. Apply bold styling to the text, by dragging to select the words [**User Name**] and clicking the **Font** button for the **Header**. Choose **Bold** from the **Font Style** list then click **OK**.

To print the page numbers at the bottom of each page in the middle as specified in step 5, click in the middle section of the **Footer**. Type **Page**, press ⌑Space⌑, click the ⌑#⌑ button, type / then click the ⌑⌑ button.
Print the date and time of printing in the top right of each page by first clicking in the right section of the **Header**. Click ⌑1·2⌑, press ⌑Space⌑, type **at**, press ⌑Space⌑ and click the ⌑⌑ button.

Confirm these headers and footers by clicking **OK**.

Print the calendar for the two weeks following this week by clicking the ⌑ tool and selecting the **Weekly Style** from the **Print style** frame. Open the **Start** list and click the date of the first day of the next week. Open the **End** list to click the date for the last day of the second week following your start date. Click **OK** to start printing.

▦ 6. To save the calendar for the following month as a Web page in the MOUS Outlook 2000 folder, open the **Outlook Shortcuts** by clicking the corresponding button and choose the **Calendar** folder before choosing **File - Save as Web Page**.

Open the **Start date** list and choose the first day of next month. Open the **End date** list to choose the last day of next month.

Deactivate the **Include appointment details** option in the **Options** frame so that comments are not shown with the calendar items in the Web page.

To choose the picture you want for the Web page background, activate the **Use background graphic** option and click the **Browse** button. Select the folder that contains your picture then the picture itself and click **Select**.

Enter the calendar's title by selecting the text in the **Calendar title** text box, pressing `Del` and typing **Management Committee Calendar**.

Click the **Browse** button next to the **File name** box to choose the calendar's name and where to save it. Open the **Save in** list and select the drive where the MOUS Outlook 2000 folder is then double-click the **MOUS Outlook 2000** folder to open it. Click in the **File name** text box and type **Committee Calendar** before clicking **Select**.

To view the Web page in your browser as soon as it is saved, make sure the **Open saved web page in browser** option is active.

Save the calendar as a Web page by clicking **Save**. Once you have viewed the Web page, close your browser window by clicking ⊠.

OTHER FOLDERS
Lesson 4.1: Contacts

OTHER FOLDERS
Lesson 4.1: Contacts

1 ▪ Accessing the Contacts

*The **Contacts** folder is where you can keep all kinds of information about your correspondents (names, addresses, telephone numbers and so on).*

▪ In the **Outlook** bar, click the **Outlook Shortcuts** group and choose the **Contacts** folder.

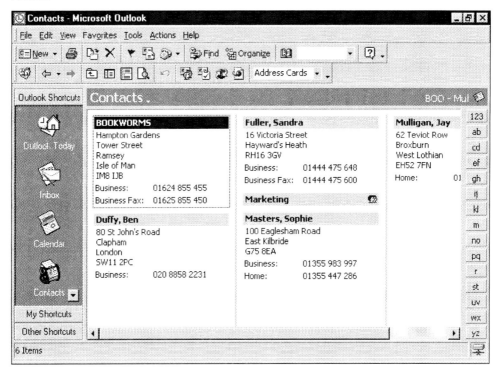

By default, the contacts are shown in Address Cards view.

▪ To access the different contacts, use the horizontal scroll bar and/or click one of the letter tabs you can see in the right of the window to go to the first contact for the selected letter.

▪ Use **View - Current View** or open the **Current View** list ┌Address Cards ▾┐ ▾ to change the view.

⊞2 ▪ Creating a contact

▪ In the **Outlook** bar, click the **Outlook Shortcuts** group and choose the **Contacts** folder.

▪ There are three ways to create a new contact:

- **File - New - Contact** or `Ctrl` **N**

- **Actions - New Contact** or `Ctrl` **N**

- Click the `⊆≡ New ▾` button.

▪ Enter your contact's details in the **General** tab:

- enter his or her **Full Name** in the corresponding text box or click the **Full Name** button to enter each element of the name.

- give his or her **Job title** and the name of the **Company** in the corresponding text boxes.

- In the **File as** list, choose how you want to store the contact. By default, Outlook takes the contact's surname followed by their first name.

- for each address you want to enter, click the `▼` button to select the address type (**Business, Home, Other**). Type the **Address** in the corresponding text box or click the **Address** button to fill out the different elements of the address.

- give the different telephone numbers in the corresponding text boxes.

- you can have up to three **E-mail** addresses for each contact. To enter the second or third e-mail address, click the `▼` button, choose **E-mail 2** or **E-mail 3** as appropriate then enter the address in the associated text box.

- if necessary, type the address of an Internet page (a URL) in the **Web page address** box. To see the page, either click the hyperlink or use **Actions - Explore Web Page**.

- add any comments about the contact in the big text box.

- if necessary, you can link the current contact (the principal contact) to other contacts using the **Contacts** button.

- if need be, indicate the categories in which the contact should be stored by typing the category in the **Categories** text box or by clicking the **Categories** button to choose one.

- you can activate the **Private** option if you do not want other people who can access your **Contacts** folder to see this item.

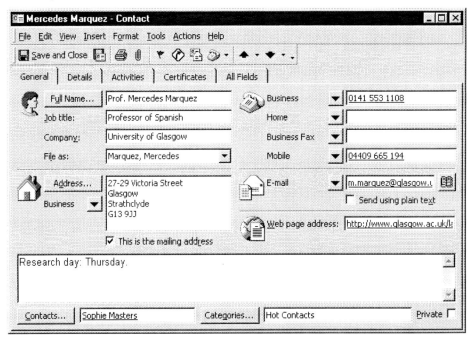

* On the **Details** page, you can add extra information about the contact:

- give any professional information: **Department**, **Office**, **Profession**, **Manager's name**, **Assistant's name**.

- enter personal details: **Spouse's name**, **Birthday**, **Nickname**, **Anniversary**.

*Under the **Activities** tab you can show items associated with the contact (such as messages, tasks or appointments).*

▪ Add your new contact to the address book using one of the following buttons:

Save and Close   to save the contact and close the window.

    to save the contact and create a new one.

Contacts appear as address cards by default, filed by their surname then first name.

▪ To make changes to a contact, double-click the contact in question. Make the changes then click Save and Close.

▪ To delete a contact, select the contact in question and press Del: the contact is moved to the **Deleted Items** folder.

To search for a contact and open the contact window, type the contact's name, surname or part of the surname in this box 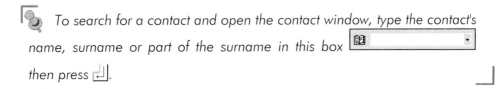 *then press .*

3 ▪ Sorting contacts

▪ In the **Outlook** bar, click the **Outlook Shortcuts** group and choose the **Contacts** folder.

▪ **View - Current View - Customize Current View**

▪ Click the **Sort** button.

*When the **Sort** dialog box opens you will notice that you can use four different sort criteria simultaneously.*

▪ For each sort criterion:

- select the name of the field by which you want to sort. If the field you want is not available, open the **Select available fields from** list and choose **All Contact Fields**.

- indicate whether you want to sort in **Ascending** or **Descending** order by activating the appropriate option.

The items are sorted according to the first sort criterion. When that value is the same for several contacts, they are then sorted by the second criterion, and so on.

❋ Click **OK**.

If you have chosen to sort by a field that is not shown in the current view, Outlook asks if you want to show it:

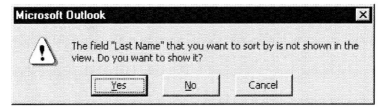

❋ Click **Yes** to show the field or **No** if you do not want to show it.

❋ Click **OK** in the **View Summary** dialog box.

 *You can remove one or more sort criteria using **View - Current View - Customize Current View** then clicking the **Sort** button: to delete one criterion, choose **(none)** in the appropriate list; delete all the criteria by clicking the **Clear All** button.*

4 ▪ Classing contacts by category

Associating a category with a contact

❋ Select the contact which you want to put into a category.

❋ **Edit - Categories**

*If you are creating or editing a contact, click the **Categories** button.*

❋ To use an existing category, tick the most appropriate option in the list.

* You can create a new category by typing its name in the **Item(s) belong to these categories** box and clicking the **Add to List** button.

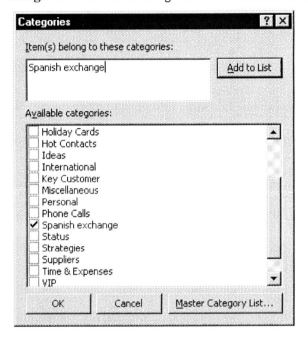

The new category is created and ticked automatically.

* Click **OK**.

Viewing contacts by their categories

* Choose to view contacts by their categories using **View - Current View - By Category**.

  The contacts are grouped according to their category and each category is preceded by a plus sign (+).

* You can expand/collapse all the categories at once by using **View - Expand/Collapse Groups** and, depending on what you want to do, clicking **Collapse All** or **Expand All**.

* To expand one category, select it and use **View - Expand/Collapse Groups - Expand This Group** or click the [+] button before the category's name.

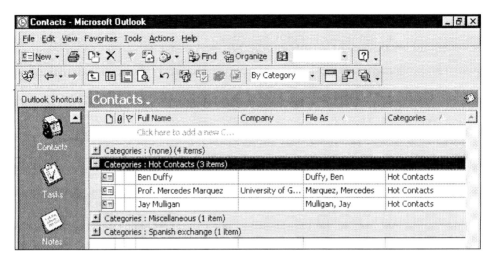

All the contacts in the category appear.

* Collapse a category using **View - Expand/Collapse Groups - Collapse This Group** or click the ⊟ in front of the category in question.

🗎 *To see all the text in each column, increase the column width by double-clicking the vertical line at the right of the column header in question.*

5 ▪ Printing the contacts

* If necessary, select the contacts you want to print. Hold down the Shift key as you click to select adjacent contacts, or the Ctrl key for non-adjacent ones.

* **File - Print** or 🖨 or Ctrl **P**

* Select the **Print style** you want from the corresponding list.

* Choose the **Print range** by activating the **All items** option or the **Only selected items** option in the corresponding frame. If you have selected **Memo Style** as the print style, only the selected items will be printed and the **Print range** frame

is replaced by the **Print options** frame, in which you can choose to **Start each item on a new page** and/or **Print attached files with item(s)**.

▪ Use the **Number of pages** list in the **Copies** frame to choose whether you want to print even pages, odd pages, or both.

▪ Enter the number of copies you want to print in the **Number of copies** text box in the **Copies** frame.

▪ Activate the **Collate copies** option for the copies to be printed copy by copy and not page by page.

▪ Click **OK** to start printing or choose to see a **Preview** by clicking the corresponding button.

> *The **Page Setup** button in the **Print** dialog box (or in the print preview window) allows you to define the page setup (paper format, headers and footers etc) for the selected print style.*

■ Linking an item to a contact

Some items are naturally linked to particular contacts, but you can also link contacts to any existing item or one you are about to create.

Linking an existing item to a contact

▪ In the **Outlook** bar, click the **Outlook Shortcuts** group and choose the **Contacts** folder.

▪ Select the contact in question or double-click it to open it.

▪ **Actions - Link - Items**

▪ In the **Look in** list and select the folder that contains the item you want to link with the contact.

▪ In the **Items** list, click the item you want.

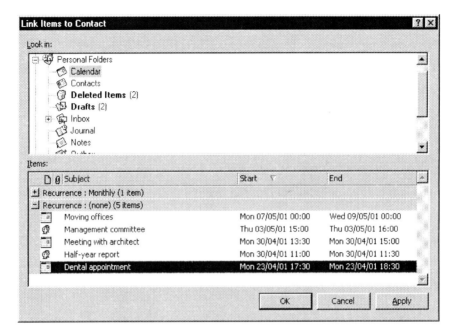

∗ Click **OK**.

∗ If you have opened the contact, click 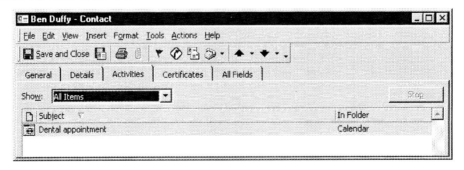 .

Viewing items linked with a contact

∗ Open the contact in question by double-clicking it.

∗ Click the **Activities** tab.

You can see a list of all the items that are linked to the contact, both items linked as described above and items where the link is automatic.

* If you only want to see certain items, open the **Show** list and click the option for the type of item you want to see.

* Once you have finished viewing the items linked with the contact, click ☒ to close the contact window.

📄 *To link other contacts to a contact you are creating, click the **Contacts** button in the dialog box and choose the contacts you want.*

📖7 ▪ Manually creating a journal entry

*The Outlook **Journal** keeps a record of your computer's activity: telephone calls, reception of messages and also the creation and editing of Microsoft Office files.*

The Journal notes where the files are saved. It is an additional tool to help you manage your own activity, or that of a department or even a company.

Manually saving an Outlook item or an Office document in the Journal

* To save an Outlook item in the Journal, select the folder that contains the item (such as the Inbox or Calendar).

* To save an Office document in the Journal, open the Windows Explorer (by right-clicking the **Start** button then choosing **Explore**) and, if necessary, click the 🖻 button to reduce the window size before selecting the drive then folder that contains the document.

Click the Outlook item or Office document and drag it to the **Journal** folder in the **My Shortcuts** group. If the Journal folder is not visible on the screen, drag the selected item or document onto the **My Shortcuts** button on the Outlook bar to open the group's contents then, without releasing the mouse button, drag your selection to the **Journal** folder.

* If need be, change the **Subject**, the **Entry type** and/or the **Company**.

- If necessary, open the first **Start time** list to change the starting date of the Journal entry.

- If necessary, open the second **Start time** list to change the starting time of the Journal entry.

- Select the **Duration** of the entry in the corresponding list.

- Use the **Contacts** button to link the entry to one or more contacts, if necessary.

- Specify the category in which the entry should be classed by typing the category's name in the **Categories** text box or by clicking the **Categories** button to select one.

- Activate the **Private** option if you do not want this entry to be seen by other people who can access your **Journal**.

- Click ![Save and Close].

- To view your journal entries, open the **Journal** folder in the **My Shortcuts** group. If necessary, click **No** to the message asking if you want Outlook to create automatic Journal entries; activate the **Please do not show this dialog again** option if you do not want to see the message the next time you access the Journal.

- To open a Journal entry, click the plus sign (+) to the left of the **Entry Type** group it is saved in.

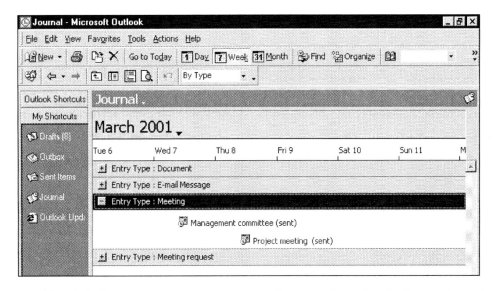

Double-click the entry you want to open; when you have finished consulting the entry, click ⊠ to close it.

Manually saving an activity in the journal

You can create a journal entry without using an existing item.

- In the **Outlook** bar, click the **My Shortcuts** group then the **Journal** folder.

- If necessary, click **No** to the message asking if you want to define automatic journal entries.

- **File - New - Journal Entry** or **Actions - New Journal Entry** or ⌷Ctrl⌷ **N**.

- In the **Subject** text box, type a description of the entry.

- Select the **Entry type** which best corresponds to the entry from the corresponding list.

- If necessary, enter the name of the company associated with the entry in the **Company** text box.

- If need be, open the first **Start time** list to change the starting date of the journal entry.

- If need be, open the second **Start time** list to change the starting time of the journal entry.

- Select the **Duration** of the entry from the corresponding list.

- Use the **Contacts** button to link one or more contacts to the entry, if necessary.

- Specify the category in which the entry should be classed by typing the category's name in the **Categories** text box or by clicking the **Categories** button to select it.

- Activate the **Private** option if you do not want this entry to be seen by other people who can access your **Journal**.

- Click 📷 Save and Close .

8 ▪ Sending contact information by e-mail

You can send a contact to other people using your e-mail.

- Select the contacts you want to send. Hold down the [Shift] key as you click to select adjacent contacts, or the [Ctrl] key for non-adjacent ones.

- **Actions - Forward** or [Ctrl] **F**

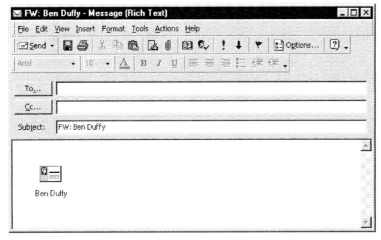

The contact (o contact appear(s) as an icon in the big message text box.

▪ Choose the recipients, change the message subject if you want to and, if necessary, add your comments in the large text box before clicking ⌐≡ Send.

 To see the contents of the contact, the recipient must open the message then double-click the contact icon.

*To add this contact to his or her **Contacts** folder, the recipient will need to drag the contact icon from the open message to his or her **Contacts** folder in the **Outlook Shortcuts** group.*

*You can also send a contact to other people by creating a message while in your **Inbox** folder and inserting the contact into your message using **Insert - Items**.*

9 ▪ Managing a distribution list

*A **distribution list** contains several contacts. When you send a message to a distribution list, you are actually choosing all the list members as recipients for your message.*

Creating a distribution list

▪ In the **Outlook** bar, click the **My Shortcuts** group then the **Contacts** folder.

▪ **Actions - New Distribution List**

▪ **File - New - Distribution List** or **Actions - New Distribution List** or ⌐Ctrl⌐ ⌐Shift⌐ **L**

*You can use the **File - New - Distribution List** command in any folder.*

▪ Type the list's name in the **Name** text box.

▪ Click the **Select Members** button.

▪ Open the **Show Names from the** list to choose the address book that contains the people you want to add as members.

» Add a member by double-clicking his or her name in the **Type name or select from list** list or by selecting his or her name and clicking **Add**.

» Add several members by selecting their names and clicking **Add**; select adjacent names by dragging or by `Shift`-clicking; to select non-adjacent names, use the `Ctrl` key.

You can select your members from different address books.

» Click **OK**.

*The **Distribution List** window appears again. Each member of the list is shown along with his or her **E-mail** address.*

» If necessary, click the **Notes** tab and enter your comments about the distribution list.

» Click [**Save and Close**].

*Distribution lists are saved in the **Contacts** folder by default. In Address Cards view they are marked with this symbol: [ ].*

To see the contents of a distribution list, double-click its name in the **Contacts** folder.

Editing a distribution list

▪ In the **Outlook** bar, click the **My Shortcuts** group then the **Contacts** folder.

▪ Double-click the distribution list you want to edit.

▪ To add a contact from an address book to the list, click the **Select Members** button, select the member as you did when you were creating the list then click **OK**.

▪ If you want to add a new member who is not in an address book, click the **Add New** button and enter the member information.

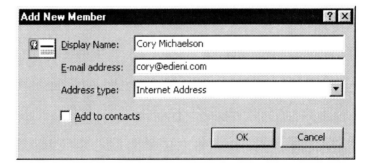

If you activate the **Add to Contacts** option the member will be added to your **Contacts** folder; if you do not, the member will only be present in the distribution list.

Click **OK**.

▪ To remove a member from the list, click his or her name and click **Remove**.

▪ Double-click a member's name to see his or her properties.

▪ When you have finished your changes, click [💾 Save and Close].

10 ▪ Adding a member to the Outlook address book

*The Outlook address book is created automatically from the addresses in your **Contacts** folder which include an e-mail address or "fax number". However, you can always add a member to the Outlook address book without using the Contacts folder.*

⁜ **Tools - Address Book** or 📖 or ⌈Ctrl⌉ ⌈Shift⌉ **B**

⁜ **File - New Contact** or 🖳

⁜ Open the **In the** list and choose **Contacts**.

Remember that the other address books, in particular the global address list, are managed by the administrator; you cannot add members to these lists.

⁜ Select the **New Contact** option from the **Select the entry type** list box then click **OK**.

⁜ Enter the details for the contact you are adding to the Outlook address book in the same way as for a contact (see Creating a contact - Chapter 4.1 Contacts).

*Be careful because you must enter either an e-mail address or fax number. If you do not, the contact will not be added to the Outlook address book but only to your **Contacts** folder.*

⁜ Click 💾 Save and Close .

⁜ Close the **Address Book** window by clicking ☒.

*The new contact is added to the Outlook address book and the **Contacts** folder.*

11 ▪ Managing your personal address book

Creating a personal address book

The personal address book can be customised. You can use it to store your personal contacts and distribution lists.

▪ **Tools - Services**

▪ Click the **Services** tab.

▪ Click the **Add** button.

▪ Select **Personal Address Book** from the **Available in formation services** list and click **OK**.

▪ If necessary, click the **Personal Address Book** tab.

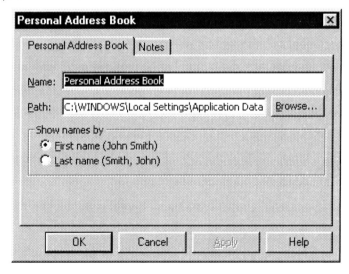

▪ If necessary, change the **Name** of the personal address book in the corresponding text box.

Personal Address Book is the default name for the personal address book.

▪ If need be, type the **Path** for this personal address book in the corresponding box or click the **Browse** button to select it.

* Activate the option that corresponds to how you want to display the names in the **Show names by** frame.

* Click **OK**.

* Click **OK** to the message that tells you that you need to restart Outlook.

* Click **OK** in the **Services** dialog box.

* Close **Outlook 2000**. Do this by clicking the [X] button or use **File - Exit**.

* Restart **Outlook 2000** by clicking the **Start** button, clicking the **Programs** option and choosing **Microsoft Outlook**.

Adding members to the Personal Address Book

* **Tools - Address Book** or [📖] or [Ctrl] [Shift] **B**

* **Tools - Options**

* Select the **Personal Address Book** from the **Keep personal addresses in** list and click **OK**.

* Open the **Show names from** list and select the address book that contains the members you want to add to the personal address book.

* Select the member(s) in question; select adjacent members by dragging or by [Shift]-clicking; to select non-adjacent members use the [Ctrl] key.

* **File - Add to Personal Address Book** or [📖]

* Close the **Address Book** window by clicking [X].

Adding a personal distribution list to the Personal Address Book

* **Tools - Address Book** or [📖] or [Ctrl] [Shift] **B**

* **File - New Entry** or [📖]

* Open the **In the** list and choose the **Personal Address Book**.

- Choose the **Personal Distribution List** option from the **Select the entry type** list then click **OK**.

- Type the list's **Name** in the corresponding text box then click **Add/Remove Members**.

- Open the **Show Names from the** list and choose the address book that contains the names you want to add to the list.

- To add a member, double-click his or her name in the **Type Name or Select from List** list or select and click the [Members ->] button.

- Add several members by selecting their names and clicking the [Members ->] button.

- Click **OK**.

  *Each member of the distribution list appears in the **Personal Distribution List** window.*

- If necessary, click the **Annotations** tab and type any comments about the list then click **OK**.

- Close the **Address Book** window by clicking the [X] button.

  *To delete members or distribution lists from one of your custom address books, go into the address book concerned, select the item(s) and use **File - Delete** or [X] or [Ctrl][Shift] **D** or [Del].*

Below you can see **Practice exercise 4.1**. This exercise is made up of 11 steps. If you do not know how to complete one of the steps, go back to the lesson to refer to the corresponding title. When you have finished, check your work by reading the **Solution** on the next page.

Steps that are likely to be tested on the exam are marked with a symbol. It is however recommended that you follow the whole exercice in order to gain a complete understanding of the lesson.

👉 **Practice exercise 4.1**

1. Go to the **Contacts** folder. Change the view in the **Contacts** folder to show the contacts grouped by category. Now return to the **Address Cards** view.

2. Create these 3 contacts:

   - <u>1st contact</u>

     Mr. Jack Madison
     Company: ULTIMA
     Business address: 63 Ennismore Terrace, London
     Postal code: SW6 1AX
     Business telephone: 020 5155 6985
     E-mail address: jmadison@edieni.com

   - <u>2nd contact</u>

     Freya Jackson
     Company: MID-NET
     Business address: 5 Ashburn Gardens, Birmingham
     Postal code: B11 2PL
     Business telephone: 0121 644 9007
     Business fax: 0121 644 9001
     E-mail address: f.jackson@edieni.com

- 3rd contact

Stephen Wilkinson
Home address: 41 Caledonia Park, Inverurie
Region: Aberdeenshire
Home telephone: 01467 332 815
E-mail address: swilkinson@edieni.com
Birthday: 25/05/1970

3. Sort the **Contacts** folder in ascending order according to the **Last Names** then in ascending order according to **First Names**.

4. Put **Jack Madison** and **Freya Jackson** into **Business** category and **Stephen Wilkinson** into the **Personal** category.

Change the view in the Contacts folder to **By Category** and expand the **Business** category.

Finish by returning to the **Address Cards** view.

5. Print the **Jack Madison** and **Freya Jackson** contacts as e-mail messages. These messages should be printed on one page and you should print two copies.

6. Link the **Management committee** meeting to **Freya Jackson**.

7. Save the **Jack Madison** contact in the Journal manually, without changing the information shown.

8. Send the **Jack Madison** and **Freya Jackson** contacts by e-mail to the recipient of your choice (one addressee in the **To** field). The **Subject** of the message should be **MADISON and JACKSON (contacts)** and you do not need to add any comments to the message.

If you are unable to send this message to another person, send it to yourself.

9. Create a distribution list that you should call **S/PHOTO** and add **Jack Madison**, **Freya Jackson** and **Stephen Wilkinson** as members.

   Now delete **Stephen Wilkinson** from the **S/PHOTO** distribution list.

10. Add this member to the Outlook address book:

    Mr. Brian Gayle
    Company: ULTIMA
    Business address: 63 Ennismore Terrace, London
    Postal code: SW6 1AX
    Business telephone: 020 5155 6986
    E-mail address: bgayle@edieni.com

11. If it has not already been done, add the Personal Address Book to your address books, keeping the default name and path, and the names display. Now add **Stephen Wilkinson** (in the Outlook address book) to the Personal Address Book and go on to delete **Stephen Wilkinson** from the Outlook address book.

If you want to put what you have learned into practice in a real document, you can work on the summary exercise 4 for the OTHER FOLDERS section that you can find at the end of this book.

It is often possible to perform a task in several different ways, but here only the quickest solution is presented. Go back to the lesson to see the other techniques that can be used.

Solution to exercise 4.1

1. To go to the Contacts folder, open the **Outlook Shortcuts** group by clicking the corresponding button on the **Outlook** bar then click the **Contacts** folder.

   To change the view in the Contacts folder so that the contacts appear grouped by category, use **View - Current View** then click **By Category**.

   Return to the Address Cards view using **View - Current View** and choose the **Address Cards** option.

2. To create the first contact, open the **Outlook Shortcuts** group by clicking the corresponding button on the **Outlook** bar then click the **Contacts** folder then the ⌞New ▾⌝ button. Make sure the **General** tab in the **Contact** dialog box is selected. Click the **Full Name** button; select **Mr.** from the **Title** drop-down list, type **Jack** in the **First** text box, type **Madison** in the **Last** text box then click **OK**. Click in the **Company** text box and type **ULTIMA**. Click in the **Business** telephone number text box (in the top right part of the dialog box) and type **020 5155 6985**. Click the **Address** button and type **63 Ennismore Terrace** in the **Street** text box, type **London** in the **City** text box, type **SW6 1AX** in the **ZIP/Postal code** box then click **OK**.

   Click in the **E-mail** text box and type **jmadison@edieni.com**. Click ⌞💾 Save and Close⌝ to create the contact.

To create the second contact, click the ⎡**New** ▾⎤ button and make sure the **General** tab in the **Contact** dialog box is selected. Click the **Full Name** button, type **Freya** in the **First** text box, type **Jackson** in the **Last** text box then click **OK**. Click in the **Company** text box and type **MID-NET**. Click in the **Business** telephone number text box (in the top right part of the dialog box) and type **0121 644 9007**. Click in the **Business Fax** text box and type **0121 644 9001**. Click the **Address** button and type **5 Ashburn Gardens** in the **Street** text box, in the **City** text box, type **Birmingham**, type **B11 2PL** in the **ZIP/Postal code** text box then click **OK**. Click in the **E-mail** text box and type **f.jackson@edieni.com**. Create the contact by clicking ⎡**Save and Close**⎤.

To create the third contact, click the ⎡**New** ▾⎤ button and make sure the **General** tab in the **Contact** dialog box is selected. Click the **Full Name** button, type **Stephen** in the **First** text box, type **Wilkinson** in the **Last** text box then click **OK**. Click in the **Home** telephone number box (in the top right part of the dialog box) and type **01467 332 815**. Click the ▾ button under the **Address** button and choose **Home**. Click the **Address** button, type **41 Caledonia Park** in the **Street** text box, type **Inverurie** in the **City** text box, type **Aberdeenshire** in the **State/Province** text box then click **OK**. Click in the **E-mail** text box and type **swilkinson@edieni.com**.

Click the **Details** tab and type **25/05/1970** in the **Birthday** text box. Create the contact by clicking ⎡**Save and Close**⎤.

3. To sort the Contacts folder in ascending order according to the Last Names then in ascending order according to the First Names, first make sure the **Contacts** folder in the **Outlook Shortcuts** group is selected. Use **View - Current View - Customize Current View** and click the **Sort** button.

Open the list in the **Sort items by** frame, scroll down the list and click the **Last Name** option. Open the list in the **Then by** frame, scroll down the list and click the **First Name** option. Make sure the **Ascending** option is active for both the criteria then click **OK**. Click **Yes** when you are asked if you want to show the **Last Name** field and click **Yes** when you are asked if you want to show the **First Name** field. Click **OK** in the **View Summary** dialog box.

4. To associate the Business category with Jack Madison, make sure the **Contacts** folder (**Outlook Shortcuts** group) is selected. Select the **Madison, Jack** contact and use **Edit - Categories**. In the **Available categories** list, activate the **Business** option then click **OK**.

To associate the Business category with Freya Jackson, select the **Jackson, Freya** contact and use **Edit - Categories**. In the **Available categories** list, activate the **Business** option then click **OK.**

To associate the Personal category with Stephen Wilkinson, select the **Wilkinson, Stephen** contact and use **Edit - Categories**. Scroll down the **Available categories** list and activate the **Personal** option then click **OK**.

To display the contents of the Contacts folder by category, use **View - Current View - By Category** then click the button in front of the **Business** category.

Return to Address Cards view by **View - Current View - Address Cards**.

5. Print the Jack Madison and Freya Jackson contacts as e-mail messages by clicking the **Jack Madison** contact, holding down the Ctrl key, clicking the **Freya Jackson** contact, then clicking the button.

Select the **Memo Style** option from the **Print style** frame and make sure **Start each item on a new page** is not active so that the messages are printed on the same page.

To print two copies, type **2** in the **Number of copies** text box in the **Copies** frame.

Start printing by clicking **OK**.

6. To link the Management committee meeting to Freya Jackson, make sure the **Contacts** folder in the **Outlook Shortcuts** group is selected. Click the **Freya Jackson** contact to select it and use **Actions - Link - Items**.

   Select the **Calendar** folder in the **Look in** list. Click the ⊟ button to the left of the **Recurrence: (none)** group in the **Items** box and select the meeting with **Management committee** as the subject.

   Click **OK** to link this item to the Freya Jackson item.

7. To save the Jack Madison contact in the Journal without changing any of the existing information, make sure the **Contacts** folder (**Outlook Shortcuts** group) is selected. Click the **Jack Madison** contact then drag to the **My Shortcuts** button on the Outlook bar to open this group's contents and, without releasing the mouse button, move the mouse to the **Journal** folder then release the mouse button.

   Save the item manually by clicking 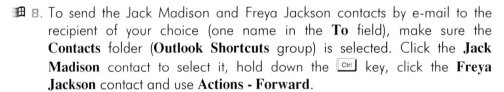 .

8. To send the Jack Madison and Freya Jackson contacts by e-mail to the recipient of your choice (one name in the **To** field), make sure the **Contacts** folder (**Outlook Shortcuts** group) is selected. Click the **Jack Madison** contact to select it, hold down the Ctrl key, click the **Freya Jackson** contact and use **Actions - Forward**.

   Click in the **To** field and type the recipient's name. Click in the **Subject** box and type **MADISON and JACKSON (contacts)**.

   Click the Send button to send the message.

9. To create a distribution list called S/PHOTO, containing Jack Madison, Freya Jackson and Stephen Wilkinson as members, make sure the **Contacts** folder in the **Outlook Shortcuts** group is selected and use **File - New - Distribution List**. Click in the **Name** text box and type **S/PHOTO** then click the **Select Members** button.

Open the **Show Names from the** list and choose the **Contacts** address book. In the **Type Name or Select from list** list, double-click **Freya Jackson (E-mail), Jack Madison (E-mail)** then **Stephen Wilkinson (E-mail)** and click **OK**. Finish by clicking [💾 Save and Close].

To delete the Stephen Wilkinson member from the S/PHOTO distribution list, double-click the **S/PHOTO** list in the **Contacts** folder, select **Stephen Wilkinson (E-mail)**, click the **Remove** button then click [💾 Save and Close].

10. To add a new member to the Outlook address book as described in step **10**, use **Tools - Address Book** and click the [🖻] tool. Open the **In the** list and choose the **Contacts**. Select the **New Contact** option in the **Select the entry type** list and click **OK**.

Click the **Full Name** button, select **Mr.** from the **Title** drop-down list, type **Brian** in the **First** text box, type **Gayle** in the **Last** text box then click **OK**. Click in the **Company** text box and type **ULTIMA**. Click in the **Business** telephone number text box (in the top right part of the dialog box) and type **020 5155 6986**. Click the **Address** button, type **63 Ennismore Terrace** in the **Street** text box, type **London** in the **City** text box, type **SW6 1AX ZIP/Postal code** text box then click **OK**. Click in the **E-mail** text box and type **bgayle@edieni.com**. Add the contact to the Outlook address book by clicking [💾 Save and Close].

Close the **Address Book** window by clicking [✖].

11. To add the Personal Address Book to your address books, use **Tools - Services** then click the **Add** button. Select the **Personal Address Book** option in the **Available information services** list and click **OK**. Click the **Personal Address Book** tab, leave the default options in this page and click **OK**. Click **OK** to the message telling you that you must restart Outlook then click **OK** in the **Services** dialog box. Use **File - Exit** to close Outlook 2000.

Click the **Start** button, choose the **Programs** menu then click the **Microsoft Outlook** option to restart Outlook 2000.

To add Stephen Wilkinson to the Outlook address book, use **Tools - Address Book** then **Tools - Options**. Select the **Personal Address Book** option from the **Keep personal addresses in** list then click **OK**. Open the **Show names from the** list and choose **Contacts**. Select the **Stephen Wilkinson (E-mail)** contact and use **File - Add to Personal Address Book**. Close the **Address Book** window by clicking ☒. To delete Stephen Wilkinson from the Outlook address book, use **Tools - Address Book**. Open the **Show names from the** list and choose the **Contacts** address book. Select **Stephen Wilkinson**, press Del then click **Yes**. Finish by closing the **Address Book** by clicking ☒.

1 ▪ Accessing the Tasks folder

❋ In the **Outlook** bar, click the **Outlook Shortcuts** group then the **Tasks** folder.

*You can also see tasks in the **Calendar** folder if **Day/Week/Month** view (**View-Current View - Day/Week/Month**) is active.*

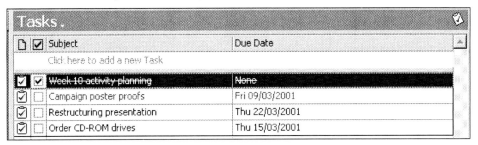

*Overdue tasks appear coloured red. Tasks preceded by an empty check box are **tasks in progress**. Tasks that are preceded by a ticked check box and are greyed and have a line through them are **completed tasks**.*

 *You can change the colours used for **Overdue** and **Completed** tasks in the **Task Options** dialog box (**Tools - Options - Preferences** tab - **Tasks Options** button).*

2 ▪ Creating a task

*A **task** is a personal or professional undertaking that you need to track until its completion.*

❋ In the **Outlook** bar, click the **Outlook Shortcuts** group then the **Tasks** folder.

❋ There are three ways to create a task:

- **File - New - Task** or Ctrl **N**

- **Actions - New Task** or Ctrl **N**

- Click the ☑ New ▾ button.

❊ Click in the **Subject** text box and type a brief description of the task.

❊ If the task has a due date, choose the **Start date** from the corresponding list then choose the end date from the **Due date** list.

❊ Choose an importance level for the task by selecting one of the options from the **Priority** list: **Low**, **Normal** or **High**.

❊ If you want to set an alarm for the current task, make sure the **Reminder** option is active and use the two associated lists to choose the date and time at which the alarm should go off.

If the default reminder time is not convenient for you, you can customise it in the **Reminder time** *list in the* **Options** *dialog box (***Tools - Options - Preferences** *tab).*

❊ In the large text box, give information or instructions relevant to the task.

❊ You can, if need be, associate this task with some **Contacts** using the corresponding button.

❊ If necessary, indicate the category in which you want to place the task in the **Categories** text box, or click the **Categories** button to select one.

❊ Activate the **Private** option if you do not want this item to be seen by other people who can access your **Tasks** folder.

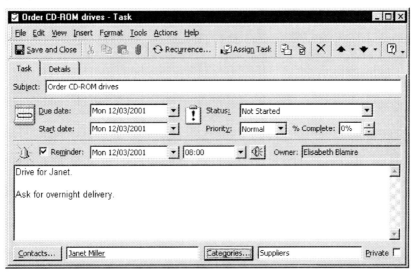

- Confirm the task by clicking the **Save and Close** button.

> You can also create a task by clicking in the **Click here to add a new Task** box. If you click this box once, your task will only have a subject; by double-clicking the box you will open the standard task creation window.

3 ▪ Creating a recurring task

- While you are creating the task, or when it is open for editing, use **Actions - Recurrence** or **Recurrence...** or **Ctrl G**.

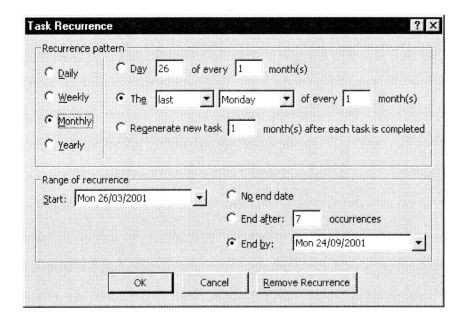

* Use the different options in the **Recurrence pattern** frame to indicate how often the task should be repeated. If you want to repeat a task as soon as it has been completed, activate the **Regenerate new task** option and specify how many **day(s), week(s) month(s)** or **year(s) after each task is completed** the task should be repeated.

* Now use the options in the **Range of recurrence** frame to indicate the period over which the task should be repeated:

No end date   the recurring item is repeated indefinitely.

End after n occurrences the task is repeated for the number of occurrences specified in the text box.

End by   ends the recurrence task on the date entered in the text box.

* If need be, choose the **Start** date of the task using the corresponding list in the **Range of recurrence** frame.

* Click **OK**.

* Click the [🖫 Save and Close] button.

> *You can remove a task's recurrence by clicking the **Remove Recurrence** button in the **Task Recurrence** dialog box (**Actions - Recurrence**).*

4 • Tracking a task's progress

Only a task's owner can track it.

* Open the task whose progress you want to track by double-clicking its subject.

* Enter a percentage in the **% Complete** text box to indicate the percentage of progress on the task.

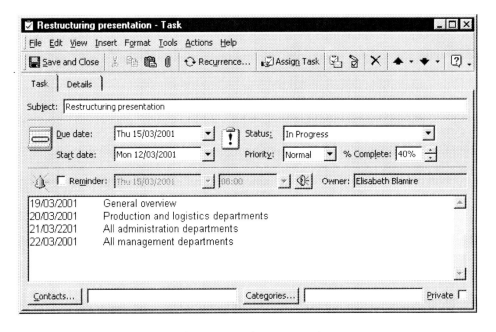

*As soon as you confirm this information, the **Status** changes to **In Progress**.*

※ If necessary, change the task's progress **Status** by choosing an appropriate option from the list.

※ To indicate that the task is finished, type **100** in the **% Complete** text box or select **Completed** in the **Status** list, or click the ⌧ tool on the **Standard** toolbar in the dialog box.

※ Confirm by clicking ⊞ Save and Close.

If another person assigned the task you have completed to you, they are informed of its completion.

📄 *If you only want to see completed tasks, activate **View - Current View - Completed Tasks**.*

You can indicate a task's completion without opening it; simply click the empty tick box that precedes the task's name.

5 ▪ Assigning a task to others

* While you are creating the task, or while you have it open for editing, use **Actions - Assign Task** or Assign Task .

* In the **To** field, type the address(es) of the person (people) to whom you want to assign the current task or click the **To** button and select them from an address book.

* If necessary, change the **Subject**, the **Start date** and **Due date**, the **Status**, the **Priority** and the **% Complete** for this task, which you are assigning to another person.

* If need be, type any extra instructions necessary for completing the task in the large text box.

* Choose whether you want to **Keep an updated copy of this task on my task list** and if you want Outlook to **Send me a status report when this task is complete** by activating the corresponding options.

* Send the task by clicking Send .

 If you have programmed a reminder, Outlook tells you that it has been deactivated as you are no longer the owner of the task.

* If necessary, click **OK**.

The creator of the task can see it in their **Tasks** folder preceded by this symbol ▣; in his or her **Sent Items** folder, the task appears like this ▣ and is preceded by the words **Task Request**. The recipient sees the task like this ▣ in his or her **Inbox**, which indicates a task request; in his or her **Tasks** folder it is preceded by this symbol: ▣.

You can also send tasks to one or more people from your **Contacts** folder. To do this, go to the **Contacts** folder and select the contact(s) to whom you want to send the task. Activate the **Actions - New Task for Contact** command. Create the task, click the ▣ Assign Task button and finish assigning the task as usual.

6 ▪ Replying to a task request

▪ Select the **Tasks** folder and double-click the task (which appears in bold) or select the **Inbox** folder and double-click the message that contains the task request.

▪ Reply to the task request by clicking ✔ Accept to accept the task, the ✗ Decline button if you want to refuse the task, or the ▣ Assign Task button if you want to pass the task to another person.

▪ Choose one of these two options:

Edit the response before sending if you want to add a comment to your reply.

Send the response now to send the response without adding a comment.

▪ If you have chosen to add a comment to your reply, do so then click ⬚Send.

*Once you accept it, the task disappears from your **Inbox** and appears in the **Tasks** folder, preceded by this symbol: ⬚. It is also placed in the **Sent Items** folder, accompanied by this symbol: ⬚. You are now the task's owner. When you refuse a task, it appears in your **Sent Items** folder accompanied by this symbol: ⬚. The person who sent you the task request is informed of your decision by a message received in his or her **Inbox**, preceded by this symbol ⬚ if the task has been accepted or this symbol ⬚ if the task has been declined. If an assigned task is refused, it becomes ownerless!*

7 ▪ Tasks folder views

*The views let you see the contents of the **Tasks** folder in different ways.*

▪ In the **Outlook** bar, click the **Outlook Shortcuts** group then the **Tasks** folder.

▪ Use **View - Current View** or open the **Current View** tool list
Simple List.

▪ Click the option for one of these views:

Simple List to see a list with a minimum of details, making it easy to see which tasks are complete.

Detailed List to see a list containing details for each task, such as its priority and how close it is to completion.

Active Tasks to see a list of unfinished tasks (including overdue ones).

Next Seven Days to see a list of tasks that are due within the next seven days.

Overdue Tasks	to show a list of overdue tasks.
By Category	to see a list of the tasks grouped according to category and sorted according to their due dates inside each category.
Assignment	to see a list containing only those tasks that have been assigned to somebody else. The list is sorted by the owner and by due date.
By Person Responsible	for a list of tasks grouped by owner and sorted according to their due date for each owner.
Completed Tasks	to see a list that contains only those tasks that are completed.
Task Timeline	to see a list of tasks as icons on a timeline, according to their start dates. Tasks without a start date are placed according to their due dates.

8 ▪ Turning an Outlook item into a task

▪ Click the Outlook item concerned and drag it to the **Tasks** folder in the **Outlook Shortcuts** group; if you cannot see the **Tasks** folder, drag the item to the **Outlook Shortcuts** button on the **Outlook** bar to show this group's contents and, without releasing the mouse button, drag the item to the **Tasks** folder.

The task creation window opens straight away.

▪ If necessary, specify this new task's characteristics (see Creating a task - parties in this chapter).

▪ Confirm the task by clicking 💾 Save and Close.

9 ▪ Classing tasks by category

Associating a category with a task

▪ Select the tasks with which you want to associate a category.

▪ **Edit - Categories**

*While you are creating or editing a task, you can click the **Categories** button.*

▪ To use an existing category, activate the one which is most appropriate for the task. You can create a new category by typing its name in the **Item(s) belong to these categories** text box and clicking the **Add to List** button.

The category you have just created is ticked automatically.

▪ Click **OK**.

Viewing tasks grouping by category

▪ Activate the By Category view using **View - Current View - By Category**.

The tasks are grouped according to category and each category is preceded by a plus sign (+).

▪ You can expand/collapse all the groups at once by activating **View - Expand/Collapse Groups** and clicking the **Collapse All** option or the **Expand All** option, whichever is appropriate.

▪ To expand one category, select it and use **View - Expand/Collapse Groups - Expand This Group** or click the ⊞ button in front of the name of the group in question.

▪ You can collapse one group by selecting the group and using **View - Expand/Collapse Groups - Collapse This Group** or by clicking the ⊟ in front of the group's name.

Below you can see **Practice exercise 4.2**. This exercise is made up of 9 steps. If you do not know how to complete one of the steps, go back to the lesson to refer to the corresponding title. When you have finished, check your work by reading the **Solution** on the next page.

Steps that are likely to be tested on the exam are marked with a ▦ symbol. It is however recommended that you follow the whole exercice in order to gain a complete understanding of the lesson.

☞ Practice exercise 4.2

1. Go to the **Tasks** folder.

 2. Create a task with the following information:

- the task's subject is **Restructuring presentation**.

- the task is to start on the Monday after today.

- the **Due date** for the task is the Thursday after next Monday.

- you do not need to set an alarm to remind you about this task.

- the instructions for the completion of the task are:

1st day	General overview
2nd day	Production and logistics departments
3rd day	All administration departments
4th day	All management departments

3. Create a recurring task which you should program for the first working day of each month starting from next month, to run for six months. This recurring task should contain the following information:

- the task's subject is **Activity sheets**.

- the instructions for the task are:

Ask each team member for last month's activity sheet.

Open the Activity sheet.xls file and save it as Activity sheet month/year.xls (e.g.: Activity sheet January/2001.xls).

Enter each team member's information.

Print the file contents.

Send the print-out to Anna Cassidy.

- a reminder dialog box should appear at **10:00** on the task's due day.

4. Change the percentage of completion of the **Restructuring presentation** task to **10%**.

5. Create the task described below and assign it to the person of your choice:

- the task's subject is **Summary of overdue payments**.

- the task's start date is the Tuesday after today.

- the **Due date** for the task is the Wednesday after next Tuesday.

- you do not need to set an alarm for this task.

- the task instructions are as follows:

Only include payments overdue by more than 15 days.

Any payments overdue by more than 2 months to be followed up by phone.

- An updated copy of the task should be stored in your Tasks folder and you want to receive a message telling you when the task is complete.

If you are unable to assign a task to another person, you cannot complete this step.

6. Before you complete this step, you need to go to another computer and create a task. This task is for next Friday and you should send it to yourself and one other person. The task should contain the following information:

- the subject is **Office supplies order**.

- a reminder dialog box should appear at **10:00** on the task's due day.

- the task instructions are as follows:

Make an inventory of supplies.

Use inventory to make up an order.

Send the inventory to Purchasing.

Send the order to Guy Preston.

Once you have sent the task request you should return to your computer.

Send a positive reply to the task request you have just sent yourself. The reply does not need commenting.

7. Change the view in the **Tasks** folder to display a list of tasks that are due in the next seven days.

Return to the **Simple List** view in the **Tasks** folder.

8. Before you complete this step, you will need to create an appointment, scheduled for a week from now, with the following information:

- the appointment's subject is **Management committee**.

- the appointment will take place in the **Harris Room**.

- the appointment should begin at **15:00** and end at **16:00**.

- you do not need to set an alarm to remind you about this appointment.

Take the appointment you have just created and turn it into a task, adding the information below to the task:

- distribute last meeting's minutes to participants before midday.

- prepare information about the restructuring project.

9. Add the **Presentation creation** category to the **Restructuring presentation** task and the **Miscellaneous** category to the **Office supplies order** and **Summary of overdue payments** tasks.

Now display the contents of the Tasks folder **By Category** and expand the **Miscellaneous** group.

Finish by returning to the **Simple List** view.

If you want to put what you have learned into practice in a real document, you can work on the summary exercise 4 for the OTHER FOLDERS section that you can find at the end of this book.

It is often possible to perform a task in several different ways, but here only the quickest solution is presented. Go back to the lesson to see the other techniques that can be used.

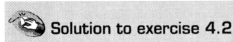 **Solution to exercise 4.2**

1. Open the Tasks folder by clicking the **Outlook Shortcuts** group in the **Outlook** bar, then clicking the **Tasks** folder.

2. To create the task shown in step 2, make sure the **Tasks** folder in the **Outlook Shortcuts** group is selected then click the [☑ New ▾] button.

   Click in the **Subject** text box and type **Restructuring presentation**.

   Open the **Start date** list and select the date of the following Monday.

   Open the **Due date** list and select the date of the Thursday after next Monday.

   Deactivate the **Reminder** option because you do not want an alarm to remind you about this task.

   Click in the large text box and type **1st day**, press the [⇥] key, type **General overview**, press [↵], type **2nd day**, press the [⇥] key, type **Production and logistics departments**, press [↵], type **3rd day**, press [⇥], type **All administration departments**, press [↵], type **4th day**, press [⇥] and type **All management departments**.

   Click the [💾 Save and Close] button to create the task.

3. To create a recurring task that you should program for the first working day of each month, starting next month and lasting six months, first make sure the **Tasks** folder in the **Outlook Shortcuts** group is selected then click the [☑ New ▾] button then the [↻ Recurrence...] button.

Activate the **Monthly** option in the **Recurrence pattern** frame then the **The** option in the same frame. Choose **first** in the first drop-down list after the **The** option and then choose **weekday** in the second list. Make sure that **1** is visible in the **of every n month()s** text box.

Open the **Start** list in the **Range of recurrence** frame and select the date of the first working day of next month.

Type **6** in the **End after n occurrences** text box in the **Range of recurrence** frame then click **OK**.

Click in the **Subject** text box and type **Activity sheets**.

Click in the large text box and type **Ask each team member for last month's activity sheet**, press ⏎, type **Open the Activity sheet.xls file and save it as Activity sheet month/year.xls (e.g.: Activity sheet January/2001.xls)**, press ⏎, type **Enter each team member's information**, press ⏎, type **Print the file contents**, press ⏎ and type **Send the print-out to Anna Cassidy**.

Make sure the **Reminder** option is active. Now check that the date in the first **Reminder** list is the date of the first working day of next week then select **10:00** in the next list.

Finish by clicking [💾 Save and Close] to create the recurring task.

4. To indicate that the **Restructuring presentation** task is 10% complete, make sure the **Tasks** folder in the **Outlook Shortcuts** folder is selected and double-click the task with **Restructuring presentation** as the subject

Select the contents of the **% Complete** text box, type **10** then click [💾 Save and Close].

5. To create the task described in step 5 of the exercise, make sure the **Tasks** folder in the **Outlook Shortcuts** group is selected then click the [✓ New ▾] button.

Click in the **Subject** text box and type **Summary of overdue payments**.

Open the **Start date** list and select the date of next Tuesday.

Open the **Due date** list and choose the date of the Wednesday after next Tuesday.

Deactivate the **Reminder** option because you do not need to program an alarm for this task.

Click in the big text box, type **Only include payments overdue by more than 15 days.**, press ⏎ and then type **Any payments overdue by more than 2 months to be followed up by phone**.

Assign the task to the person of your choice by clicking the ⌨ Assign Task button. Click in the **To** field and type the name of the person to whom you want to assign the task. Make sure the **Keep an updated copy of this task on my task list** and **Send me a status report when the task is complete** options are active.

Send the task by clicking ⌨ Send .

6. To send a positive reply to the task request you have created using another computer, open the **Outlook Shortcuts** group by clicking the corresponding button on the **Outlook** bar and click the **Inbox** folder. Double-click the **Task Request: Office supplies order** message. Click the ✔ Accept button, activate the **Send the response now** option and click **OK**.

7. To change the view in the Tasks folder so that only tasks that are due in the next seven days are shown, use **View - Current View** and click the **Next Seven Days** option.

Return to the Simple List view in the Tasks folder by activating **View - Current View** and clicking the **Simple List** option.

8. To change the appointment you have created into a task, open the **Outlook Shortcuts** group by clicking the corresponding button on the **Outlook** bar and click the **Calendar** folder. Now, in the Date Navigator, select the date of the day one week from now.

In the Diary, place the mouse pointer to the left of the **Management committee** item and, when the mouse pointer takes this shape ✛ , drag it to the **Tasks** folder in the **Outlook Shortcuts** group.

Add the instructions given in step 8 to this new task by clicking in the large text box. Type **distribute last meeting's minutes to participants before midday**, press ⏎ and type **prepare information about the restructuring project**.

Create this new task by clicking 🖫 Save and Close.

9. To associate the "Presentation creation" category to the task called Restructuring presentation, make sure the **Tasks** folder in the **Outlook Shortcuts** group is selected. Select the **Restructuring presentation** task and use **Edit - Categories**. Type **Presentation creation** in the **Item(s) belong to these categories** box, click the **Add to List** button then click **OK**.

Associate the "Miscellaneous" category to the Office supplies order task by selecting the **Office supplies order** task and activating **Edit - Categories**. Activate the **Miscellaneous** option in the **Available categories** list and click **OK**.

To associate the "Miscellaneous" category to the Summary of overdue payments task, select the **Summary of overdue payments** task and activate **Edit - Categories**. Activate the **Miscellaneous** option in the **Available categories** list and click **OK**.

OTHER FOLDERS
Lesson 4.3: Notes

1 ▪ Creating a note

> **Notes** are the electronic equivalent of the Post-it® notes that you can stick everywhere.

▪ On the **Outlook** bar, click the **Outlook Shortcuts** group then the **Notes** folder.

▪ There are three ways to create a note:

  - **File - New - Note** or <kbd>Ctrl</kbd> **N**

  - **Actions - New Note** or <kbd>Ctrl</kbd> **N**

  - Click the 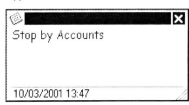 button.

▪ Type the note's text.

```
┌────────────────────────────┐
│ ▨ ▮▮▮▮▮▮▮▮▮▮▮▮▮▮▮▮      ☒ │
│ Stop by Accounts           │
│                            │
│                            │
│                            │
│ 10/03/2001 13:47          ╱│
└────────────────────────────┘
```

▪ Click the ☒ button to close the note window.

2 ▪ Reading/editing a note

▪ On the **Outlook** bar, click the **Outlook Shortcuts** group then the **Notes** folder.

▪ Double-click the note you want to read or edit.

```
┌────────────────────────────┐
│ ▨ ▮▮▮▮▮▮▮▮▮▮▮▮▮▮▮▮      ☒ │
│ Stop by Accounts before 3 pm. │
│                            │
│                            │
│ 10/03/2001 13:48          ╱│
└────────────────────────────┘
```

▪ Close the note window by clicking .

📄 *To change the size of the note window, place the mouse pointer over the window's border or in the bottom right corner of the window (the pointer becomes a two-headed arrow) and drag.*

📖3 ▪ Changing the Notes view

▪ On the **Outlook** bar, click the **Outlook Shortcuts** group then the **Notes** folder.

▪ Use **View - Current View** or open the list on the **Current View**
[Icons ▾] tool. Click the option for one of the following views:

Icons   to see the notes as icons. By default, the notes appear as
large icons ([Large Icons]) placed from left to right. You can
choose to display them as small icons ([Small Icons]) or as a
list ([List]).

Notes List   for a list of notes sorted by the date they were created.

Last Seven Days to see notes created during the last seven days.

By Category   to see the notes in a list, grouped by category and sorted by
creation date.

By Color   for a list of notes grouped by colour then sorted by creation
date within each colour.

 *You can associate a category with a note by selecting the note then activating **Edit - Categories**. If you can see the category you want in the list, activate the corresponding option. If there is no appropriate category, create one by typing its name in the **Item(s) belong to these categories** box and clicking the **Add to List** button. Confirm by clicking **OK**.*

4 ▪ Customising notes

You can change the colour, window size and the font for the notes you create.

▪ Go to the **Notes** folder and activate **Tools - Options**. Click the **Preferences** tab then the **Notes Options** button.

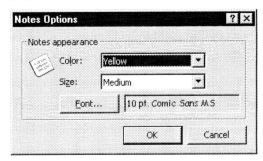

▪ To change the **Color** of notes, open the corresponding list and choose the colour you want.

▪ Change the **Size** of the notes window by opening the corresponding list and choosing the size you want: **Small**, **Medium** or **Large**.

▪ To change the appearance of the text in the notes, click the **Font** button, make your changes and click **OK**.

▪ Click the **OK** button twice.

Below you can see **Practice exercise 4.3**. This exercise is made up of 4 steps. If you do not know how to complete one of the steps, go back to the lesson to refer to the corresponding title. When you have finished, check your work by reading the **Solution** on the next page.

All the steps in this exercise are likely to be tested in the exam.

 Practice exercise 4.3

1. Create a note with the following contents:

   Stop by Accounts

2. Change the note you created in the previous step so that it reads:

   Stop by Accounts before 3pm

3. Change the view in the **Notes** folder so that the notes are shown in a list sorted by creation date.

   Return to the **Icons** view in the **Notes** folder.

4. Change the appearance of the text used in the notes by applying the **Times New Roman** font, size **11**.

If you want to put what you have learned into practice in a real document, you can work on the summary exercise 4 for the OTHER FOLDERS section that you can find at the end of this book.

It is often possible to perform a task in several different ways, but here only the quickest solution is presented. Go back to the lesson to see the other techniques that can be used.

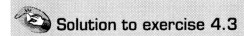 **Solution to exercise 4.3**

1. Click the **Tasks** folder then the New button. Type **Stop by Accounts** then close the note window by clicking the button.

2. Double-click the note you created in the previous step. Change the text then click the button.

3. Activate the **View - Current View** command and choose the **Notes List** option. To change the display back to Icons view, activate **View - Current View** and choose **Icons**.

4. Use **Tools - Options**, click the **Preferences** tab then the **Notes Options** button. Click the **Font** button select the **Times New Roman** option in the **Font** list, choose **11** in the **Size** list then click **OK**. Finish by clicking **OK** twice.

CONFIGURING OUTLOOK
Lesson 5.1: Managing items

🕮 1 ▪ Moving items to another folder

First method

* Select the folder that contains the items you want to move then select the items in question; use the `Shift` key to select adjacent items or the `Ctrl` key for non-adjacent items.

* **Edit - Move to Folder** or `Ctrl` `Shift` **V**

* Select the destination folder. If it does not exist, create it by clicking the **New** button.

* Click **OK**.

* If necessary, define the characteristics of the new item then click `💾 Save and Close`.

Second method

* Select the folder that contains the items you want to move then select the items in question; use the `Shift` key to select adjacent items or the `Ctrl` key for non-adjacent items.

* **Tools - Organize** or `🗂 Organize`

   The **Organize** window appears in the top of the window.

* Click the **Using Folders** tab, if need be.

* In the **Move "item" selected below to** list, select the destination folder for the selected items.

* Click **Move**.

* Close the **Organize** window by clicking the ❎ button or by clicking the `🗂 Organize` button or using **Tools - Organize**.

📄 *You cannot use this method to move items from the **Calendar** and **Journal** folders.*

2 ▪ Deleting items

Items are deleted in two steps: at the first step you move deleted items to a "bin"; at the second step you delete the items definitively. This technique means that you can recover items you have deleted by accident.

※ Select the folder that contains the items you want to move then select the items in question; use the ⟨Shift⟩ key to select adjacent items or the ⟨Ctrl⟩ key for non-adjacent items.

※ **Edit - Delete** or ⟨×⟩ or ⟨Ctrl⟩ **D**

*The items disappear from their original folder and appear in the **Deleted Items** folder.*

※ Recover items you have deleted in error by moving them to another folder (see previous heading).

※ To delete items definitively, select the **Deleted Items** folder then use **Edit - Delete** or ⟨×⟩ or ⟨Ctrl⟩ **D**.

Outlook asks you for confirmation, because you are definitively deleting the items:

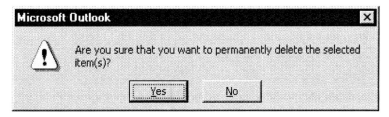

Confirm the deletion by clicking **Yes**.

*You can deactivate this confirmation message by deactivating the **Warn before permanently deleting items** option in the **Advanced Options** dialog box (**Tools - Options - Other** tab - **Advanced Options** tab).*

*You can permanently delete items from your **Deleted Items** folder using **Tools - Empty "Deleted Items" folder.** You will be asked to confirm the deletion.*

3 ▪ Putting an item into a category

▪ Select the folder then the item you want to associate with a category.

▪ **Edit - Categories**

*When you are creating or editing an item you can click the **Categories** button.*

▪ Create a new category by typing its name in the **Item(s) belong to these categories** text box and clicking the **Add to List** button.

▪ To use an existing category, click the categories that are best suited to your item in the list.

▪ Click **OK**.

4 ▪ Managing the master Outlook categories

Creating a new category

▪ Select an item and activate **Edit - Categories**.

▪ Click the **Master Category List** button.

▪ For each new category you want to create, type its name in the **New category** text box and click **Add**.

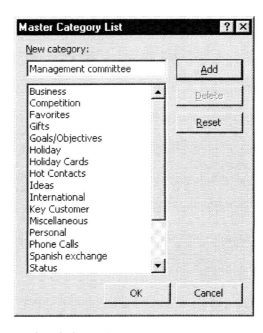

» Confirm your additions by clicking **OK**.

Deleting categories

» Select any item and activate **Edit - Categories**.

» Click the **Master Category List** button.

» For each category you want to delete, select it in the list and click **Delete**.

» You can delete all the custom categories you have created by clicking the **Reset** button then click **OK** in the message telling you that the category list will now only contain Outlook categories.

» Confirm your deletions by clicking **OK**.

5 ▪ Viewing items by category

The technique you use differs, depending on the item's type.

Non-message items

※ Go to the folder concerned and activate **View - Current View - By Category**.

※ You can expand/collapse all the categories using **View - Expand/Collapse Groups** and clicking **Collapse All** or **Expand All**.

※ To expand one category, select it and use **View - Expand/Collapse Groups - Expand This Group** or click the ⊞ button in front of the group in question.

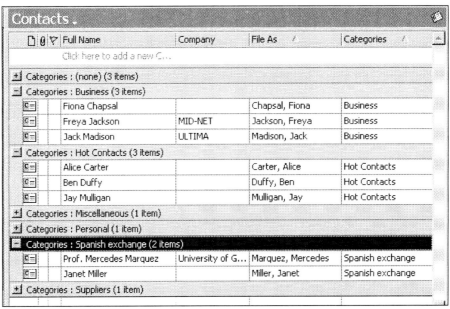

*In this example, six categories are present in the Contacts folder and three have been expanded (**Business, Hot Contacts** and **Spanish exchange**).*

※ Collapse a category by selecting it and using **View - Expand/Collapse Groups - Collapse This Group** or by clicking the ⊟ button in front of the selected category.

Messages

* Select a message folder.

* **View - Current View - Customize Current View**

* Click the **Group By** button.

* Open the **Group items by** list and choose **Categories**.

* Click **OK** twice.

* Expand and collapse the category groups using the same techniques as for non-message items (see previous subheading).

 *You can return to the previous view by activating **View - Current View - Customize Current View**, clicking the **Group By** button and choosing (none) in the **Group items by** list. Click **OK** twice.*

Below you can see **Practice exercise 5.1**. This exercise is made up of 5 steps. If you do not know how to complete one of the steps, go back to the lesson to refer to the corresponding title. When you have finished, check your work by reading the **Solution** on the next page.

Steps that are likely to be tested on the exam are marked with a ▦ symbol. It is however recommended that you follow the whole exercice in order to gain a complete understanding of the lesson.

 Practice exercise 5.1

▦ 1. Use the **Organize** window to move the message in the **Inbox** folder with **Buffet after AGM** as the subject to the **Outlook Training** folder.

2. Move the **Jack Madison**, **Freya Jackson** and **Brian Gayle** contacts to the **Deleted Items** folder. Now recover the **Jack Madison** and **Freya Jackson** contacts and activate the **Contacts** folder again. Finish by permanently deleting the **Brian Gayle** contact.

▦ 3. Associate the **Personal** category with the **Stop by accounts...** note.

▦ 4. Create a new category called **Management committee**.

▦ 5. Change the view in the **Contacts** folder to **By Category** then expand the **Business** category group.

  Finish by returning to **Address Cards** view in the **Contacts** folder.

If you want to put what you have learned into practice in a real document, you can work on the summary exercise 5, CONFIGURING OUTLOOK section that you can find at the end of this book.

It is often possible to perform a task in several different ways, but here only the quickest solution is presented. Go back to the lesson to see the other techniques that can be used.

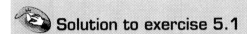

Solution to exercise 5.1

1. To use the Organize window (second method) to move the "Buffet after AGM" message from the Inbox to the Outlook Training folder, go to the **Outlook Shortcuts** group on the **Outlook** bar and click the **Inbox** folder. Click the message with **Buffet after AGM** as the subject and click the ⊞ Organize button.

   Open the **Move message selected below to** list, choose the **Outlook Training** folder and click **Move**.

   Finish by clicking the ⊞ Organize button to close the **Organize** window.

2. To move the Jack Madison, Freya Jackson and Brian Gayle contacts to the **Deleted Items** folder, go to the **Outlook Shortcuts** group on the **Outlook** bar and click the **Contacts** folder. Click **Brian Gayle**, hold down the Ctrl key and click **Freya Jackson** and **Jack Madison** then click ✕.

   Recover the **Jack Madison** and **Freya Jackson** contacts so that the Contacts folder is visible again by first selecting the **Deleted Items** folder. Click the **Freya Jackson** row and, holding down the Ctrl key, click the **Jack Madison** row. Click the ⊞ Organize button, open the **Move item selected below to** list, select the **Contacts** folder and click the **Move** button. Close the **Organize** window by clicking ⊞ Organize.

   To delete the Brian Gayle contact permanently, make sure you are in the **Deleted Items** folder and click the **Brian Gayle** row. Click the ✕ button and confirm the definitive deletion of the contact by clicking **Yes**.

3. To associate the Personal category with the "Stop by Accounts…" note, go to the **Outlook Shortcuts** group on the **Outlook** bar and click the **Notes** folder. Select the **Stop by Accounts…** note and activate **Edit - Categories**. Scroll down the **Available categories** list and activate the **Personal** choice before clicking **OK.**

4. To create a new category called Management committee, select any item and use **Edit - Categories**. Click the **Master Category List** button and type **Management committee** in the **New category** text box before clicking **Add**. Click the **OK** button twice.

5. To view the Contacts folder contents by category, first go to the **Outlook Shortcuts** group on the **Outlook** bar and click the **Contacts** folder. Activate **View - Current View - By Category** then click the ☐ button before the **Business** category group.

Return to Address Cards view by activating **View - Current View - Address Cards**.

CONFIGURING OUTLOOK
Lesson 5.2: Environment

🗐 1 ▪ **Customising the menu bar**

Renaming a menu or an option

▪ **View - Toolbars - Customize**

*You can also right-click one of the toolbars and click **Customize**.*

▪ Click the **Commands** tab.

▪ Select the menu or option you want to rename and click the **Modify Selection** button.

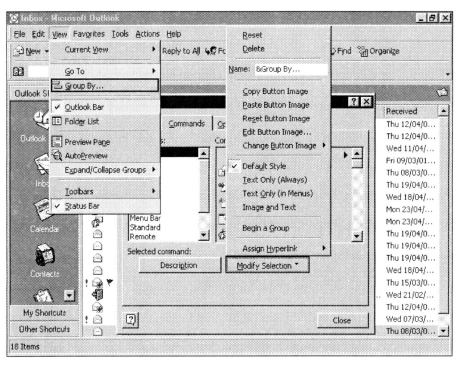

▪ Change the menu's or the option's name in the **Name** text box, remembering to type a **&** in front of the character you want to underline and press ⏎.

▪ Close the **Customize** dialog box by clicking **Close**.

Adding an option to a menu

* **View - Toolbars - Customize**

* Click the **Commands** tab.

* Open the menu to which you want to add an option, by clicking its name.

* In the **Categories** list, select the category that contains the option you want to add.

* Select the option you want to add from the **Commands** list and drag it to the appropriate position in the open menu.

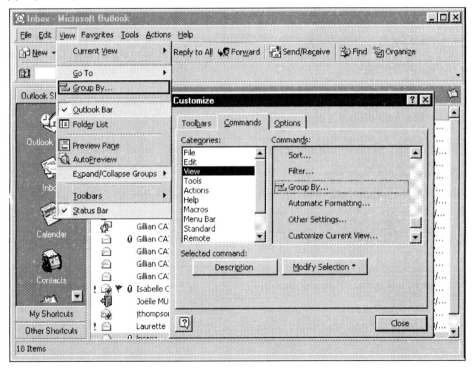

* The **Group By** option has been added to the **View** menu under the **Go To** command.

* Close the **Customize** dialog box by clicking **Close**.

Adding a new menu to the menu bar

* **View - Toolbars - Customize**
* Click the **Commands** tab.
* Select the **New menu Category** in the corresponding list.
* Select the **New menu** option in the **Commands** box and drag it to its appropriate position on the menu bar.
* Click the **Modify Selection** button and change the name of the menu in the **Name** box, typing a **&** in front of the letter to underline then press ⏎.
* Click the menu's name to open it and add the options you want (see above).
* Close the **Customize** dialog box by clicking **Close**.

Moving a menu or an option

* **View - Toolbars - Customize**
* Click the **Commands** tab.
* Select the menu or option you want to move and drag it to its new position.

In this example, the **Actions** menu is being moved to between the **View** and **Favorites** menus

* Release the mouse button when the black line (vertical for a menu, horizontal for an option) is in the right position.
* Close the **Customize** dialog box by clicking **Close**.

Deleting an option or menu

* **View - Toolbars - Customize**

* Click the **Commands** tab.

* Select the menu or option you want to delete and drag it off the menu bar or toolbar.

* Release the mouse button when a black cross appears under the mouse pointer.

* Close the **Customize** dialog box by clicking **Close**.

 To undo the changes you have made to the menu bar and restore the original settings, open the Customize dialog box (View - Toolbars - Customize) and click the Toolbars tab. Select the Menu Bar option, click the Reset button then the Yes button in the message telling you that all the changes made to the menu bar will be cancelled.

By default, the last commands you used are shown first in the menus. If you want to see all a menu's commands straight away when you click it, deactivate the Menus show recently used commands first option in the Customize dialog box (View - Toolbars - Customize - Options tab).

You can change the way in which the menus are displayed by selecting one of the options in the Menu animations list in the Customize dialog box (View - Toolbars - Customize - Options tab).

▣2 ▪ Creating an Office document without leaving Outlook 2000

Creating a document then publishing it in a message folder

※ Select a message folder (such as the **Inbox**, or **Sent Items** folder, or a folder you have created).

※ **File - New Office Document** or ⌈Ctrl⌉⌈Shift⌉ **H**

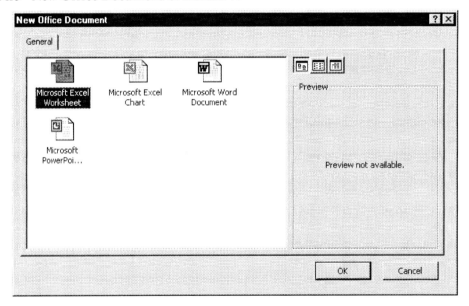

The icons you can see in this dialog box correspond to the Office programs installed on your computer.

※ Select the icon for the application in which you want to create a new document and click **OK**.

※ Make sure the **Post the document in this folder** option is active and click **OK**.

The window for the Office program corresponding to the icon you selected appears.

※ Use the application's functions to create your new document.

⚫ If necessary, save this new document on your computer. Do this by activating **File - Save As**, select the drive and folder in which you want to save the new Office document, type its **File name** in the corresponding box then click **Save**.

⚫ Click the **Post** button.

The Office document appears in the active message folder.

 *To edit an Office document, select the message folder in which it has been stored, double-click the document in question, make the necessary changes and use **File - Save** before closing it.*

Creating a document then sending it

⚫ **File - New Office Document** or Ctrl Shift **H**

⚫ Select the icon for the application in which you want to create a new document and click **OK**.

⚫ Activate the **Send the document to someone** option then click **OK**.

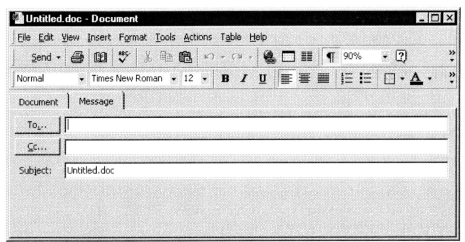

⚫ Type in the recipient(s)'s address(es) (the **To** and **Cc** fields) then, if necessary, change the **Subject** of the message in the corresponding text box.

* Click the **Document** tab and use the application's functions to create your document.

* If necessary, save this new document on your computer. Do this by activating **File - Save As**, select the drive and folder in which you want to save the new Office document, type its **File name** in the corresponding box then click **Save**.

* Click the [Send ▾] button.

🗊3 ▪ Using the Office Clipboard

*Several items can be copied to the **Office Clipboard**, unlike the **Windows Clipboard**, which can only store one item at a time.*

* Open the **Clipboard** toolbar using **View - Toolbars - Clipboard** or right-click one of the toolbars in the active window and choose **Clipboard**.

*The **Clipboard** toolbar appears automatically after the second consecutive copy.*

* For each item you want to copy or move:

  - select the item; if it is in a different application to Outlook 2000, go into the appropriate application.

  - to move something, use **Edit - Cut** or [✂] or [Ctrl] **X** and to copy something, use **Edit - Copy** or [▤] or [Ctrl] **C**.

*The selection(s) now appear(s) in the clipboard and is shown as an icon on the **Clipboard** toolbar.*

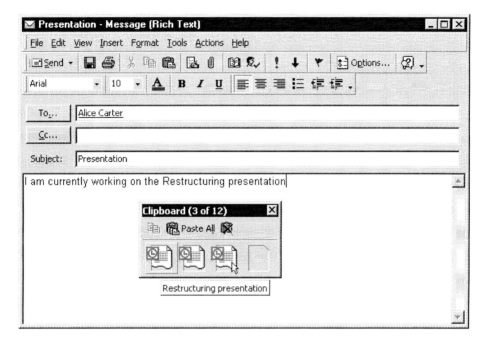

When you point to an icon (without clicking), a screen tip appears containing the first 50 characters from the cut or copied item.

- For each item you want to paste:

  - click where you want to paste the item; if you want to paste it into another item (such as a message, contact or note) from the active one, open this item; if it is to be pasted into a different program to Microsoft Outlook 2000, switch to this program.

  - on the **Clipboard** toolbar, click the icon for the item you want to paste; if the **Clipboard** toolbar has been docked, click the **Items** button to see the icons.

- Close the **Clipboard** toolbar by clicking the ☒ button or by deactivating the **Clipboard** option in the **View - Toolbars** menu.

You can store up to 12 items on the clipboard. If you try to copy/move more than 12 items, a message appears asking if you want to delete the first item on the clipboard.
This clipboard can be used in all Microsoft Office applications.

The [Paste All] button on the **Clipboard** toolbar enables you to paste all the items stored in the clipboard.

The clipboard empties when you close all your Microsoft Office applications. You can empty the clipboard yourself by clicking the [] tool on the **Clipboard** toolbar.

Below you can see **Practice exercise 5.2**. This exercise is made up of 3 steps. If you do not know how to complete one of the steps, go back to the lesson to refer to the corresponding title. When you have finished, check your work by reading the **Solution** on the next page.

All the steps in this exercise are likely to be tested in the exam.

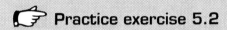 **Practice exercise 5.2**

1. Add the **Group By** option from the **View** category to the **View** menu, under the **Go To** option. Now rename this option **Group** and finish by deleting it.

2. Create an Excel document without leaving Outlook 2000 and send it to the recipient of your choice:

- the message subject is **Judy's training days for May**.

- the message contents are:

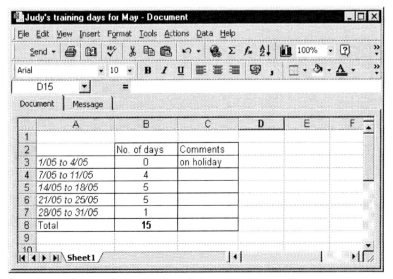

You do not need to save the new Office document on your computer.

3. Open the **Restructuring presentation** task and copy the words **General overview** and **Production and logistics departments** to the Office Clipboard.

Now create a message with the subject **Presentation** and place the items you have just copied in this message as shown below (the items from the clipboard have been underlined in the example). Finish by sending the message to the recipient of your choice:

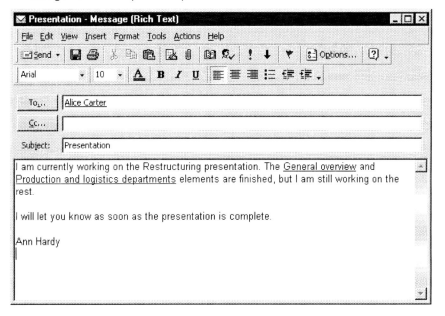

If you want to put what you have learned into practice in a real document, you can work on the summary exercise 5, CONFIGURING OUTLOOK section that you can find at the end of this book.

It is often possible to perform a task in several different ways, but here only the quickest solution is presented. Go back to the lesson to see the other techniques that can be used.

 Solution to exercise 5.2

1. To add the **Group By** option from the **View** category to the **View** menu under the **Go To** option, activate **View - Toolbars - Customize** and click the **Commands** tab. Click the **View** menu to open it and select the **View** category in the **Categories** list. Click the **Group By** option in the **Commands** list and drag it to under the **Go To** command in the **View** menu.

   Rename the **Group By** option to **Group**: first make sure the **Group By** option in the **View** menu is selected then click the **Modify Selection** button. Click in front of **By** in the **Name** text box, press ⌨Del three times then press ⏎.

   Delete the **Group** command: first make sure it is selected in the **View** menu then drag it off the menu bar and toolbars. Release the mouse when a black cross appears under the mouse pointer.

   Close the **Customize** dialog box by clicking **Close**.

2. To create an Excel document in Outlook 2000 according to the instructions given in step 2 and send it to the recipient of your choice, activate **File - New - Office Document**. Select the **Microsoft Excel Worksheet** icon and click **OK**. Choose the **Send the document to someone** option and click **OK**.

   Type the recipient's address in the **To** field. Delete the contents of the **Subject** text box and type **Judy's training days for May** in its place.

   Click the **Document** tab and use the functions in the Excel application to create the table shown in step 2.

Send the message.

⊞ 3. To open the Restructuring presentation task and copy the "General overview" and "Production and logistics departments" texts to the Office clipboard, open the **Tasks** folder. Double-click the **Restructuring presentation** task and activate **View - Toolbars - Clipboard**. Select the words **General overview**, press ⌨Ctrl **C** then select the words **Production and logistics departments** and press ⌨Ctrl **C**. Close the task window by clicking ✖.

To create a new message with Presentation as the subject, in which you will place the items you have just copied, in step 3, select the **Inbox** folder and click the 🔲New ▾ button. Click in the **To** box and type the message recipient's address. Click in the **Subject** box and type **Presentation**. In the message body, type **I am currently working on the Restructuring presentation. The**, press Space, click the first icon on the **Clipboard** toolbar, press Space, type **and**, press Space, click the second icon on the **Clipboard** toolbar, press Space, type **elements are finished, but I am still working on the rest.**, press ⏎ once, type **I will let you know as soon as the presentation is complete.**, press ⏎ and type your name.

Send the message.

█ SUMMARY EXERCISES

Summary exercise 1   OUTLOOK 2000

Display the contents of the **Drafts** folder then the **Outlook Today** folder.

Show the folder list temporarily and select the **Inbox** folder.

Show the Office Assistant then look at the help for creating a signature.

Close the help window and hide the Office Assistant.

Summary exercise 2   E-MAIL

Create two messages according to the following instructions:

- The first message can be sent to the recipients of your choice (two in the **To** field and one in the **Cc** field) and should contain the information in the screen below:

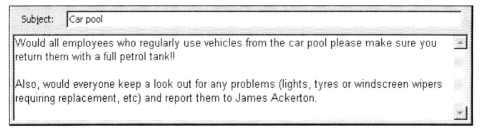

```
Subject:   Car pool

Would all employees who regularly use vehicles from the car pool please make sure you
return them with a full petrol tank!!

Also, would everyone keep a look out for any problems (lights, tyres or windscreen wipers
requiring replacement, etc) and report them to James Ackerton.
```

- The second message should be saved so that you can edit and send it later (with one recipient in the **To** field) and should resemble the screen below:

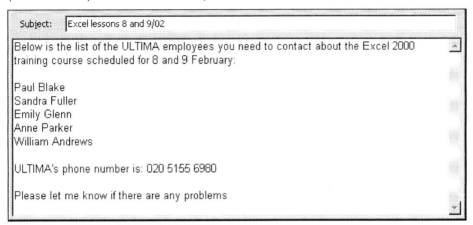

Make the changes shown below to the message in the **Drafts** folder with **Excel Lessons 8 and 9/02** as the subject so that you have a result like that in the screen below then send the message:

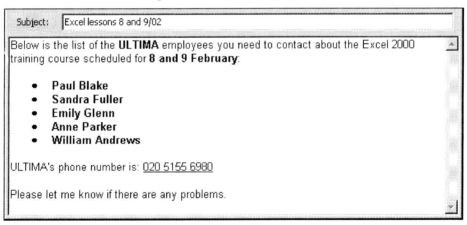

Create two signatures like these:

- **Name Surname** (apply Bold formatting)
  Tel.: 0000 000 0000 (your personal telephone number)

Call this signature **Personal**.

- **Name Surname** (apply Bold formatting)
  Tel.: 0000 000 0000 (your professional telephone number)
  email: name@company.com (your e-mail address)

Call this signature **Professional**.

Neither of these signatures should be the default signature.

Create a new message like the one shown here:

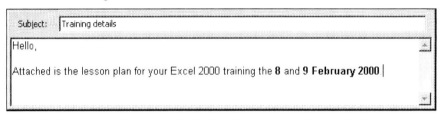

Now insert the **Summary 2.doc** file from the **Summary** folder in the **MOUS Outlook 2000** folder as an attachment.

Under the attachment, insert your signature called **Professional** then send the message to the recipient of your choice.

Create the message shown below and select the recipients from an address book (at least two names in the **To** field):

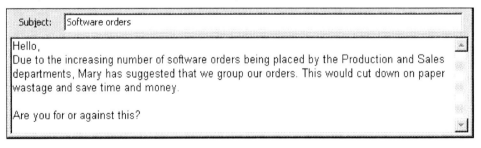

Insert a follow up flag to tell the recipients that you expect a reply within seven days at the latest.

Define **For** and **Against** voting buttons.

Define the tracking options for the message so that you are alerted when the recipients read the message then send the message.

Change the **Celebration** message sent previously so that it resembles the screen below then resend it without changing the recipients:

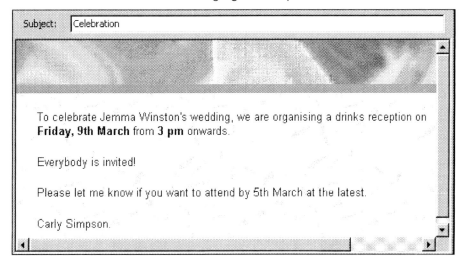

Create and send the messages shown below to yourself from another computer. If you cannot use another computer, create and send these messages from your own computer.

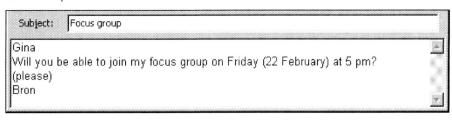

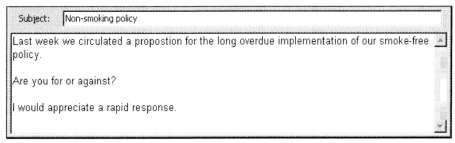

You should define **For** and **Against** voting buttons for the second message.

Return to your own computer and reply to the sender of the **Focus group** message you have just received:

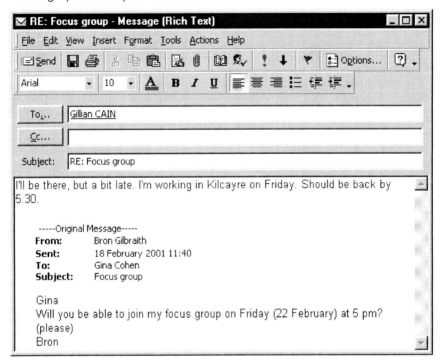

Send your message and close the original message window.

Open the message you have received with **Non-smoking policy** as the subject and reply to the sender by voting **For**. You do not need to add comments to your reply before sending it.

Forward this message to the recipient of your choice without adding any comments then close the original message window.

Use the menu method to sort the messages in the **Inbox** in ascending order of sender (**From** field) then in ascending order of date of reception (**Received** field).

Now use the mouse to sort the messages in the **Inbox** in descending order of date of reception (**Received** field).

Use the menu method to group the messages in the **Inbox** folder in ascending order of sender (**From** field) then in descending order of date of reception (**Received** field); the grouping fields should be visible on the screen.

Expand all the groups at once. Now collapse one group then all the groups at once. Finish by removing all the groups.

Print the contents of the **Non-smoking policy** and **Focus group** messages on different pages.

Search the **Inbox** folder for the message whose subject contains the text **Focus** then close the **Find** window.

Change the view in the **Inbox** folder by doing the following:

- Add a **Size** column to the right of the **From** column.

- Add a **Cc** column to the right of the **Size** column.

- Centre the contents of the **Size** and **Cc** columns.

- Change the label of the **Cc** field to **Copy**.

- Delete the **Copy** and **Size** columns.

Create **Training** and **Personal** folders in the **Sent Items** folder, but do not add shortcuts to these folders to the **Outlook** bar.

Now rename the **Personal** folder **Others** and copy the **Software orders**, **Training details** and **Non-smoking policy** messages from the **Sent Items** folder to the **Training** folder. Check the contents of the **Training** folder then close the folder list.

Summary exercise 3   THE CALENDAR

Create an event scheduled for next **Wednesday** and **Thursday**, with the following contents:

- The event subject is **Trade Fair**.

- The event is to take place in **Dublin**.

- You do not need to set an alarm to remind you about this appointment.

Create a recurring appointment scheduled for the first working day of each week, starting next week and to run for four weeks. The appointment should contain the following information:

- The subject of the recurring appointment is **Project leaders' meeting**.

- The appointment will take place in **My office**.

- The appointment should begin at **9:00** and end at **10:30**.

- A dialog box reminding you of the appointment should appear **10 minutes** before it is due to start.

Create a meeting at another computer. Schedule this meeting seven days from now and choose yourself (your presence is required) and another person (whose presence is optional) as attendees. The meeting should contain this information:

- The meeting should begin at **13:30** and end at **14:30**.

- The subject of the meeting is **Sales strategy planning**.

- It is to take place in the **Conference room**.

- A dialog box reminding you of this meeting should appear **15 minutes** before it is due to begin.

Send the meeting request to the attendees and return to your own computer.
Now send a positive reply to the meeting request without adding any comments.

Define the following page setup characteristics for the **Weekly Style** printing style:

- The days of the week should be shown in a grid on the page.

- Each week should be printed on one page.

- You should include the task list and a blank area for notes.

- Define the time range for printing as follows: start time at **7:30** and end time at **19:00**.

Now, for the same print style, define margins of **1 cm** at the top, bottom, right and left of the page and choose the **Landscape** orientation. Delete all the default footers and create new headers and footers as follows:

- The page numbers should be printed in the middle of the bottom of each page like this: **Page [Page #]/[Total pages]**.

- The date and time of printing are to appear at the top right of each page as follows: **the [Date printed] at [Time printed]**.

Finish by printing the calendar for the two weeks after this week.

Summary exercise 4   OTHER FOLDERS

Create these 4 contacts:

<u>1st contact</u>

Philip Coggan
Company: Standard World
Office address: 18-22 Mint Road, Lincoln, LN1 1UD
Region: Lincolnshire
Office phone: 01522 526 520
E-mail: pcoggan@edieni.com

<u>2nd contact</u>

Danielle Winters
Company: Standard World
Office address: 18-22 Mint Road, Lincoln, LN1 1UD
Region: Lincolnshire1
Office phone: 01522 526 525
Office fax: 01522 526 529
E-mail: dwinters@edieni.com

<u>3rd contact</u>

Isla Brennan
Company: Standard World
Office address: 18-22 Mint Road, Lincoln, LN1 1UD
Region: Lincolnshire
Office phone: 01522 526 523
E-mail: ibrennan@edieni.com

<u>4th contact</u>

Alan Packer
Home address: 90 Bermondsey Street, London, SE1 3UB
Home phone: 020 9937 4519
E-mail: apacker@edieni.com
Birthday: 17/03/1966

Associate the **Desktop software** category with the **Philip Coggan** and **Danielle Winters** contacts and the **Programming** category with the **Isla Brennan** contact.

Display the contents of the **Contacts** folder **By Category** and expand the group for the **Desktop software** category then return to **Address Cards** view.

Print the **Philip Coggan**, **Danielle Winters** and **Isla Brennan** contacts as e-mail messages on one page.

Manually save the **Isla Brennan** contact in the Journal, leaving the default information in the entry.

Use e-mail to send the **Philip Coggan** and **Danielle Winters** contacts to the recipient of your choice (one name in the **To** field). The **Subject** of the message should be **COGGAN and WINTERS (contacts)** and you do not need to add any comments to the message.

Create a distribution list called **DT/SOFT** and add the members **Philip Coggan**, **Alan Packer** and **Danielle Winters**.
Now delete **Alan Packer** from the **DT/SOFT** distribution list.

If it has not already been done, add the Personal Address Book to your address book list, leaving the default name, path and display mode for the names. Now, add **Alan Packer** (in the Outlook Address Book) to the Personal Address Book then delete this contact from the Outlook Address Book.

Create a task with the following information:

- The task's subject is **Update training requirements**.

- The task's start date is next **Monday**.

- The end date (**Due date**) for the task is the **Wednesday** after next Monday.

- You do not need to set an alarm to remind you about this task.

- The instructions for the task are as follows:

1st day	Update desktop software requirements
2nd day	Update programming requirements
3rd day	Cross-check with team leader

Change the **Update training requirements** progress to **15%**.

Create the following task and assign it to the person of your choice:

- The subject of the task is **Invoices**.

- The task's start date is next **Thursday**.

- The end date (**Due date**) for the task is the **Friday** after next Monday.

- You do not need to set an alarm to remind you about this task.

- The instructions for the task are as follows:

Prepare invoices for February's training courses.

Check the payments for January and follow up late payments.

An updated copy of the task should be stored in your task list and you are to receive a message once the task is completed.

Associate the **Training** category with the **Update training requirements** task and the **Accounts** category with the **Invoices** task.

Create a note containing **Exam results**.

Change this note so that it reads:

Ask for all exam results from the team leaders

Change the appearance of the text of the notes by applying the **Comic Sans MS** font in size **10**.

Summary exercise 5   **CONFIGURING OUTLOOK**

Use the **Organize** window (second method) to move the message in the **Sent Items** folder with **Excel lessons 8 and 9/02** as the subject to the **Training** folder.

Move the **Philip Coggan, Danielle Winters** and **Alan Packer** contacts to the **Deleted Items** folder. Recover the **Philip Coggan** and **Danielle Winters** contacts so that they are present in the **Contacts** folder again, then finish by permanently deleting the **Alan Packer** contact.

Associate the **Desktop software** category with the **Ask for all exam...** note and create a new category called **Team motivation days**.

Add a menu called **Misc** to the right of the **Actions** menu and add the **Sort** and **Filter** options from the **View** category to this menu. Finish by deleting the **Misc** menu.

Microsoft Office User Specialist Outlook 2000
Table of objectives

Tasks	Lessons	Pages	Exercises	Pages
Use Microsoft Outlook 2000 Mail to Communicate with Others Inside and Outside Your Company				
Read mail	Lesson 2.2 Title 1	72	Exercise 2.2 Point 1	81
Send mail	Lesson 2.1 Title 2	26	Exercise 2.1 Point 2	55
Compose mail by entering text	Lesson 2.1 Title 3	30	Exercise 2.1 Point 3	56
Print mail	Lesson 2.3 Title 5	92	Exercise 2.3 Point 5	115
Address mail by entering text	Lesson 2.1 Title 2	26	Exercise 2.1 Point 2	55
Use mail features (forward, reply, and recall)	Lesson 2.1 Titles 12 and 13 Lesson 2.2 Titles 2 and 5	49 and 50 73 and 78	Exercise 2.1 Points 12 and 13 Exercise 2.2 Points 2 and 5	61 81 and 82
Use address book to address mail	Lesson 2.1 Title 10	45	Exercise 2.1 Point 10	60
Flag mail messages	Lesson 2.1 Title 11	47	Exercise 2.1 Point 13	61
Navigate within mail	Lesson 2.1 Title 1	26	Exercise 2.1 Point 1	55
Find messages	Lesson 2.3 Title 7	96	Exercise 2.3 Point 7	115
Configure basic mail print options	Lesson 2.3 Title 5	92	Exercise 2.3 Point 5	115

Tasks	Lessons	Pages	Exercises	Pages
Work with attachments	Lesson 2.1 Title 7	40	Exercise 2.1 Point 7	58
	Lesson 2.2 Title 4	76	Exercise 2.2 Point 4	82
Add a signature to mail	Lesson 2.1 Title 6	38	Exercise 2.1 Point 6	58
Customize the look of mail	Lesson 2.1 Titles 3 and 4	30 and 34	Exercise 2.1 Points 3 and 4	56 and 57
Use mail templates (themes) to compose mail	Lesson 2.1 Title 5	35	Exercise 2.1 Point 5	57
Integrate and use mail with other Outlook components	Lesson 2.3 Title 15	112	Exercise 2.3 Point 15	116
Customize menu and tasks bars	Lesson 5.2 Title 1	246	Exercise 5.2 Point 1	255
Use Outlook 2000 to Manage Messages				
Create folders	Lesson 2.3 Title 12	110	Exercise 2.3 Point 12	116
Sort mail	Lesson 2.3 Title 2	87	Exercise 2.3 Point 2	114
Set viewing options	Lesson 2.3 Titles 1 and 8	86 and 100	Exercise 2.3 Points 1 and 8	114 and 115
Archive mail messages	Lesson 2.3 Titles 9 to 11	106 to 110	Exercise 2.3 Points 9 to 11	115 and 116
Filter a view	Lesson 2.3 Title 6	94	Exercise 2.3 Point 6	115
Use the Outlook 2000 Calendar				
Navigate within the calendar	Lesson 3.1 Titles 2 and 3	127 and 128	Exercise 3.1 Points 2 and 3	133
Schedule appointments and events	Lesson 3.2 Title 1	136	Exercise 3.2 Point 1	149

TABLE OF OBJECTIVES

Tasks	Lessons	Pages	Exercises	Pages
Set reminders	Lesson 3.2 Titles 3 and 4	139 and 140	Exercise 3.2 Points 3 and 4	149 and 150
Print in calendar	Lesson 3.3 Titles 1 and 2	158 and 159	Exercise 3.3 Points 1 and 2	173
Schedule multi-day events	Lesson 3.2 Title 2	138	Exercise 3.2 Point 2	149
Configure calendar print options	Lesson 3.3 Titles 3 to 5	160 to 169	Exercise 3.3 Points 3 to 5	173 and 174
Customize the calendar view	Lesson 3.1 Title 4	129	Exercise 3.1 Point 4	133
Schedule recurring appointments	Lesson 3.2 Title 5	141	Exercise 3.2 Point 5	150
Customize menu and task bars	Lesson 5.2 Title 1	246	Exercise 5.2 Point 1	255
Add and remove meeting attendees	Lesson 3.2 Title 7	146	Exercise 3.2 Point 7	150
Plan meetings involving others	Lesson 3.2 Title 6	143	Exercise 3.2 Point 6	150
Save a personal or team calendar as a Web page	Lesson 3.3 Title 6	171	Exercise 3.3 Point 6	174
Book office resources directly (e.g., conference rooms)	Lesson 3.2 Title 6	143	Exercise 3.2 Point 6	150
Integrate calendar with other Outlook components	Lesson 2.1 Title 8	42	Exercise 2.1 Point 8	59
Navigate and Use Outlook 2000 Effectively				
Use Outlook Help and Office Assistant	Lesson 1.1 Title 4	18	Exercise 1.1 Point 4	22
Move items between folders	Lesson 5.1 Title 1	236	Exercise 5.1 Point 1	242
Navigate between Outlook components	Lesson 1.1 Title 2	14	Exercise 1.1 Point 2	22
Modify the Outlook Master Categories List	Lesson 5.1 Title 4	238	Exercise 5.1 Point 4	242

Tasks	Lessons	Pages	Exercises	Pages
Assign items to a category	Lesson 5.1 Title 3	238	Exercise 5.1 Point 3	242
Sort information using categories	Lesson 5.1 Title 5	240	Exercise 5.1 Point 5	242
Use the Office Clipboard	Lesson 5.2 Title 3	252	Exercise 5.2 Point 3	256
Use Contacts				
Create, edit, and delete contacts	Lesson 4.1 Title 2	181	Exercise 4.1 Point 2	200
Send contact information via e-mail	Lesson 4.1 Title 8	192	Exercise 4.1 Point 8	201
Organize contacts by category	Lesson 4.1 Title 4	184	Exercise 4.1 Point 4	201
Manually record an activity in a journal	Lesson 4.1 Title 7	189	Exercise 4.1 Point 7	201
Link activities to a Contact	Lesson 4.1 Title 6	187	Exercise 4.1 Point 6	201
Sort contacts using fields	Lesson 4.1 Title 3	183	Exercise 4.1 Point 3	201
Use Tasks				
Create and update one-time tasks	Lesson 4.2 Titles 2 and 4	210 and 213	Exercise 4.2 Points 2 and 4	220 and 221
Accept and decline tasks	Lesson 4.2 Title 6	216	Exercise 4.2 Point 6	222
Organize tasks using categories	Lesson 4.2 Title 9	219	Exercise 4.2 Point 9	223
Assign tasks to others	Lesson 4.2 Title 5	215	Exercise 4.2 Point 5	221
Create tasks from other Outlook components	Lesson 4.2 Title 8	218	Exercise 4.2 Point 8	222
Change the view for tasks	Lesson 4.2 Title 7	217	Exercise 4.2 Point 7	222

TABLE OF OBJECTIVES

Integrate Microsoft Office Applications and Other Applications with Outlook 2000 Components				
Create and use Office documents inside Outlook 2000	Lesson 2.1 Title 9	43	Exercise 2.1 Point 9	59
	Lesson 5.2 Title 2	250	Exercise 5.2 Point 2	255
Use Notes				
Create and edit notes	Lesson 4.3 Titles 1 and 2	230	Exercise 4.3 Points 1 and 2	233
Organize and view notes	Lesson 4.3 Title 3	231	Exercise 4.3 Point 3	233
Customize notes	Lesson 4.3 Title 4	232	Exercise 4.3 Point 4	233

A

C

E

E-MAIL

EVENTS

F

FIELDS

FILTERING

FINDING

FOLDER LIST

FOLDERS

FONTS

FOOTERS

G

GROUPING

H

HEADERS

HELP

INDEX

I

ITEMS

J

JOURNAL

M

MARGINS

MEETINGS

MENU BAR

MENUS

MESSAGE

N

INDEX

O

P

R

V

VIEW

VOTING

W

WEB PAGE

List of available titles in
the Microsoft Office User Specialist collection

Visit our Internet site for the list of the latest titles published.
http://www.eni-publishing.com

ACCESS 2000
EXCEL 2000 CORE
EXCEL 2000 EXPERT
EXCEL 2002 EXPERT
OUTLOOK 2000
POWERPOINT 2000
WORD 2000 CORE
WORD 2000 EXPERT
WORD 2002 EXPERT